Getting Started with Haskell Data Analysis

Put your data analysis techniques to work and generate publication-ready visualizations

James Church

BIRMINGHAM - MUMBAI

Getting Started with Haskell Data Analysis

Commissioning Editor: Amey Varangaonkar
Acquisition Editor: Trusha Shriyan
Content Development Editor: Arun Nadar
Technical Editor: Diksha Wakode
Copy Editor: Safis Editing
Proofreader: Safis Editing
Indexer: Priyanka Dhadke
Graphics: Alishon Mendonsa
Production Coordinator: Deepika Naik

First published: October 2018

Production reference: 1301018

Published by Packt Publishing Ltd.
Livery Place
35 Livery Street
Birmingham
B3 2PB, UK.

ISBN 978-1-78980-286-3

www.packtpub.com

`mapt.io`

Mapt is an online digital library that gives you full access to over 5,000 books and videos, as well as industry leading tools to help you plan your personal development and advance your career. For more information, please visit our website.

Why subscribe?

- Spend less time learning and more time coding with practical eBooks and Videos from over 4,000 industry professionals

- Improve your learning with Skill Plans built especially for you

- Get a free eBook or video every month

- Mapt is fully searchable

- Copy and paste, print, and bookmark content

Packt.com

Did you know that Packt offers eBook versions of every book published, with PDF and ePub files available? You can upgrade to the eBook version at `www.packt.com` and as a print book customer, you are entitled to a discount on the eBook copy. Get in touch with us at `customercare@packtpub.com` for more details.

At `www.packt.com`, you can also read a collection of free technical articles, sign up for a range of free newsletters, and receive exclusive discounts and offers on Packt books and eBooks.

Contributors

About the author

James Church lives in Clarksville, Tennessee, United States, where he enjoys teaching, programming, and playing board games with his wife, Michelle. He is an assistant professor of computer science at Austin Peay State University. He has consulted for various companies and a chemical laboratory for the purpose of performing data analysis work. James is the author of *Learning Haskell Data Analysis*.

Packt is searching for authors like you

If you're interested in becoming an author for Packt, please visit authors.packtpub.com and apply today. We have worked with thousands of developers and tech professionals, just like you, to help them share their insight with the global tech community. You can make a general application, apply for a specific hot topic that we are recruiting an author for, or submit your own idea.

Table of Contents

Preface

Data analysis is part computer science and part statistics. An important part of data analysis is validating your assumptions with real-world data to see whether there is a pattern, or a particular user behavior that you can validate.

In this book, we are going to learn about data analysis from the perspective of the Haskell programming language. The goal of this book is to take you from being a beginner in math and statistics, to the point that you feel comfortable working with large-scale datasets. While mathematics is a big part of data analysis, we've tried to keep this book simple and approachable so that you can apply what you learn to the real world.

Who this book is for

This book is intended for people who wish to expand their knowledge of statistics and data analysis via real-world examples. A basic understanding of the Haskell language is expected. If you are feeling brave, you can jump right into a functional programming style.

What this book covers

Chapter 1, *Descriptive Statistics*, teaches you about the Text.CSV library. It also covers some of the descriptive statistics functions, such as mean, median, and mode.

Chapter 2, *SQLite3*, focuses on how to get the data from CSV into SQLite3. You will understand the data types of SQLite3 and how to fetch data using SQL statements. It also covers how to create your own custom module of descriptive statistics.

Chapter 3, *Regular Expressions*, introduces you to regular expression syntax, such as dots and pipe. It also covers character classes at length. Finally, it teaches you how to use regular expressions within a CSV file and an SQLite3 database.

Chapter 4, *Visualizations*, starts with the installation of gnuplot and the EasyPlot Haskell library. It covers how to use moving average function to analyze stock data. Finally, it teaches you how to make publication-ready plots by adding legends and saving those plots to files.

Chapter 5, *Kernel Density Estimation*, introduces you to central limit theorem and normal distribution and helps you to understand the difference between them. Later, it talks about the kernel density estimator and how to apply it to a dataset.

Chapter 6, *Course review*, works on the MovieLens data by applying what you have learned from the first five chapters. In addition to what was covered in the earlier chapters, you will also be exploring a few more interesting techniques for analyzing the data.

To get the most out of this book

You will need to set up the IHaskell notebook environment to test the examples in these chapters. You will also need some knowledge of the Haskell programming language, math, and statistics.

Download the example code files

You can download the example code files for this book from your account at www.packt.com. If you purchased this book elsewhere, you can visit www.packt.com/support and register to have the files emailed directly to you.

You can download the code files by following these steps:

1. Log in or register at www.packt.com.
2. Select the **SUPPORT** tab.
3. Click on **Code Downloads & Errata**.
4. Enter the name of the book in the **Search** box and follow the onscreen instructions.

Once the file is downloaded, please make sure that you unzip or extract the folder using the latest version of:

- WinRAR/7-Zip for Windows
- Zipeg/iZip/UnRarX for Mac
- 7-Zip/PeaZip for Linux

The code bundle for the book is also hosted on GitHub at `https://github.com/PacktPublishing/Getting-Started-with-Haskell-Data-Analysis`. In case there's an update to the code, it will be updated on the existing GitHub repository.

We also have other code bundles from our rich catalog of books and videos available at `https://github.com/PacktPublishing/`. Check them out!

Download the color images

We also provide a PDF file that has color images of the screenshots/diagrams used in this book. You can download it here: `https://www.packtpub.com/sites/default/files/downloads/9781789802863_ColorImages.pdf`.

Conventions used

There are a number of text conventions used throughout this book.

`CodeInText`: Indicates code words in text, database table names, folder names, filenames, file extensions, pathnames, dummy URLs, user input, and Twitter handles. Here is an example: "We can see that we have the ability to download a CSV file called `table.csv`."

Any command-line input or output is written as follows:

```
sudo apt-get install sqlite3 libsqlite3-dev
```

Bold: Indicates a new term, an important word, or words that you see on screen. For example, words in menus or dialog boxes appear in the text like this. Here is an example: "We need to hit **Apply**, and then we have to hit **Apply** again."

Warnings or important notes appear like this.

Tips and tricks appear like this.

Get in touch

Feedback from our readers is always welcome.

General feedback: If you have questions about any aspect of this book, mention the book title in the subject of your message and email us at customercare@packtpub.com.

Errata: Although we have taken every care to ensure the accuracy of our content, mistakes do happen. If you have found a mistake in this book, we would be grateful if you would report this to us. Please visit www.packt.com/submit-errata, selecting your book, clicking on the Errata Submission Form link, and entering the details.

Piracy: If you come across any illegal copies of our works in any form on the internet, we would be grateful if you would provide us with the location address or website name. Please contact us at copyright@packt.com with a link to the material.

If you are interested in becoming an author: If there is a topic that you have expertise in, and you are interested in either writing or contributing to a book, please visit authors.packtpub.com.

Reviews

Please leave a review. Once you have read and used this book, why not leave a review on the site that you purchased it from? Potential readers can then see and use your unbiased opinion to make purchase decisions, we at Packt can understand what you think about our products, and our authors can see your feedback on their book. Thank you!

For more information about Packt, please visit packt.com.

Descriptive Statistics 1

In this book, we are going to learn about data analysis from the perspective of the Haskell programming language. The goal of this book is to take you from being a beginner in math and statistics, to the point that you feel comfortable working with large-scale datasets. Now, the prerequisites for this book are that you know a little bit of the Haskell programming language, and also a little bit of math and statistics. From there, we can start you on your journey of becoming a data analyst.

In this chapter, we are going to cover descriptive statistics. Descriptive statistics are used to summarize a collection of values into one or two values. We begin with learning about the Haskell `Text.CSV` library. In later sections, we will cover in increasing difficulty the range, mean, median, and mode; you've probably heard of some of these descriptive statistics before, as they're quite common. We will be using the IHaskell environment on the Jupyter Notebook system.

The topics that we are going to cover are as follows:

- The CSV library—working with CSV files
- Data ranges
- Data mean and standard deviation
- Data median
- Data mode

The CSV library – working with CSV files

In this section, we're going to cover the basics of the CSV library and how to work with CSV files. To do this, we will be taking a closer look at the structure of a CSV file; how to install the `Text.CSV` Haskell library; and how to retrieve data from a CSV file from within Haskell.

Now to begin, we need a CSV file. So, I'm going to tab over to my Haskell environment, which is just a Debian Linux virtual machine running on my computer, and I'm going to go to the website at `retrosheet.org`. This is a website for baseball statistics, and we are going to use them to demonstrate the CSV library. Find the link for **Data Downloads** and click **Game Logs**, as follows:

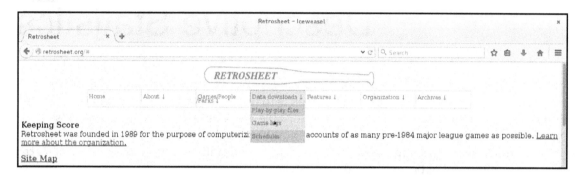

Now, scroll down just a little bit and you should see game logs for every single season, going all the way back to 1871. For now, I would like to stick with the most recent complete season, which is 2015:

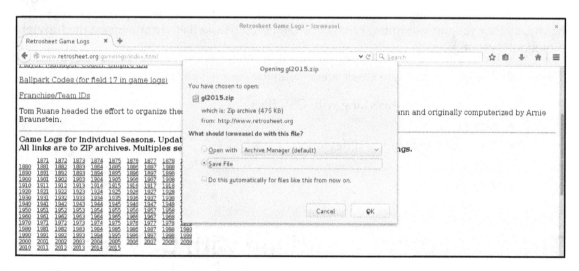

So, go ahead and click the **2015** link. We will have the option to download a ZIP file, so go ahead and click **OK**. Now, I'm going to tab over to my Terminal:

```
                         jcchurch@dataanalysis: ~/Downloads

File  Edit  View  Search  Terminal  Help
jcchurch@dataanalysis:~$ cd Downloads/
jcchurch@dataanalysis:~/Downloads$ ls
gl2015.zip
jcchurch@dataanalysis:~/Downloads$ unzip gl2015.zip
Archive:  gl2015.zip
  inflating: GL2015.TXT
jcchurch@dataanalysis:~/Downloads$ vi GL2015.TXT
```

Let's go into the `Downloads` folder, and if we hit `ls`, we see that there's our ZIP file. Let's unzip that file and see what we have. Let's open up `GL2015.TXT`. This is a CSV file, and will display something like the following:

```
                         jcchurch@dataanalysis: ~/Downloads                                ×

File  Edit  View  Search  Terminal  Help
"20150405","0","Sun","SLN","NL",1,"CHN","NL",1,3,0,54,"N","","","","CHI11",35055
,184,"110010000","000000000",36,10,3,0,0,3,0,0,0,4,1,11,4,1,0,0,10,4,0,0,0,0,27,
8,0,1,0,0,32,5,3,0,0,0,0,0,0,2,0,12,1,0,0,0,7,6,3,3,0,0,27,8,2,0,0,0,"wintm901",
"Mike Winters","wegnm901","Mark Wegner","fostm901","Marty Foster","muchm901","Mi
ke Muchlinski","","(none)","","(none)","mathm001","Mike Matheny","maddj801","Joe
 Maddon","waina001","Adam Wainwright","lestj001","Jon Lester","roset001","Trevor
 Rosenthal","hollm001","Matt Holliday","waina001","Adam Wainwright","lestj001","
Jon Lester","carpm002","Matt Carpenter",5,"heywj001","Jason Heyward",9,"hollm001
","Matt Holliday",7,"peraj001","Jhonny Peralta",6,"adamm002","Matt Adams",3,"mol
iy001","Yadier Molina",2,"wongk001","Kolten Wong",4,"jay-j001","Jon Jay",8,"wain
a001","Adam Wainwright",1,"fowld001","Dexter Fowler",8,"solej001","Jorge Soler",
9,"rizza001","Anthony Rizzo",3,"casts001","Starlin Castro",6,"coghc001","Chris C
oghlan",7,"olt-m001","Mike Olt",5,"rossd001","David Ross",2,"lestj001","Jon Lest
er",1,"lastt001","Tommy La Stella",4,"","Y"^M
@
@
@
@
@
@
@
@
"GL2015.TXT" 2429 lines, 2648768 characters
```

A CSV file is a file of comma-separated values. So, you'll see that we have a file divided up, where each line in this file is a record, and each record represents a single game of baseball in the 2015 season; and inside every single record is a listing of values, separated by a comma. So, the very first game in this dataset is a game between the St. Louis Cardinals—that's SLN—and the Chicago Cubs—that's CHN—and this game took place on March 5th 2015. The final score of this first game was 3-0, and every line in this file is a different game.

Now, CSV isn't a standard, but there are a few properties of a CSV file which I consider to be safe. Consider the following as my suggestions. A CSV file should keep one record per line. The first line should be a description of each column. In a future section, I'm going to tell you that we need to remove the header line; and you'll see that this particular file doesn't have this header line. I still like to see the description line for each column of values. If a field in a record includes a comma, then that field should be surrounded by double quote marks. Now we don't see an example of this—at least, not on this first line—but we do see examples of many values having quote marks surrounding the file, such as the very first value in the file, the date:

```
"20150405","0","Sun","SLN","NL",1,"CHN","NL",1,3,0,54,"N","","","","CHI11",35055
,184,"110010000","000000000",36,10,3,0,0,3,0,0,0,4,1,11,4,1,0,0,10,4,0,0,0,27,
8,0,1,0,0,32,5,3,0,0,0,0,0,2,0,12,1,0,0,0,7,6,3,3,0,0,27,8,2,0,0,0,"wintm901",
"Mike Winters","wegnm901","Mark Wegner","fostm901","Marty Foster","muchm901","Mi
ke Muchlinski","","(none)","","(none)","mathm001","Mike Matheny","maddj801","Joe
 Maddon","waina001","Adam Wainwright","lestj001","Jon Lester","roset001","Trevor
 Rosenthal","hollm001","Matt Holliday","waina001","Adam Wainwright","lestj001","
Jon Lester","carpm002","Matt Carpenter",5,"heywj001","Jason Heyward",9,"hollm001
","Matt Holliday",7,"peraj001","Jhonny Peralta",6,"adamm002","Matt Adams",3,"mol
iy001","Yadier Molina",2,"wongk001","Kolten Wong",4,"jay-j001","Jon Jay",8,"wain
a001","Adam Wainwright",1,"fowld001","Dexter Fowler",8,"solej001","Jorge Soler",
9,"rizza001","Anthony Rizzo",3,"casts001","Starlin Castro",6,"coghc001","Chris C
oghlan",7,"olt-m001","Mike Olt",5,"rossd001","David Ross",2,"lestj001","Jon Lest
er",1,"lastt001","Tommy La Stella",4,"","Y"^M
```

In a CSV file, if a field is surrounded by quote marks, then it is optional, unless it has a comma inside that value. While we're here, I would like to make a note of the tenth column in this file, which contains the number 3 on this particular row. This represents the away-team score in every single record of this file. Make a note that our first value on the tenth column is a 3—we're going to come back to that later on.

Our next task is installing the Text.CSV library; we do this using the Cabal tool, which connects with the Hackage repository and downloads the Text.CSV library:

```
jcchurch@dataanalysis:~/Downloads$ cabal install csv
Resolving dependencies...
cabal: Entering directory '/tmp/cabal-tmp-8375/csv-0.1.2'
Configuring csv-0.1.2...
Building csv-0.1.2...
Preprocessing library csv-0.1.2...
[1 of 1] Compiling Text.CSV        ( Text/CSV.hs, dist/build/Text/CSV.o )
Creating package registration file: /tmp/pkgConf-csv-0.18375.2
Installing library in
/home/jcchurch/.cabal/lib/x86_64-linux-ghc-7.6.3/csv-0.1.2-HemIOijiMwyGSAMWRDOxZ
A
Registering csv-0.1.2...
cabal: Leaving directory '/tmp/cabal-tmp-8375/csv-0.1.2'
Installed csv-0.1.2
jcchurch@dataanalysis:~/Downloads$ █
```

The command that we use to start the install, shown in the first line of the preceding screenshot, is cabal install csv. It takes a moment to download the file, but it should download and install the Text.CSV library in our home folder. Now, let me describe what I currently have in my home folder:

```
jcchurch@dataanalysis:~/Downloads$ cd ..
jcchurch@dataanalysis:~$ ls
Code      Documents  Dropbox  Pictures  Templates
Desktop   Downloads  Music    Public    Videos
jcchurch@dataanalysis:~$ cd Code/
jcchurch@dataanalysis:~/Code$ ls
HaskellDataAnalysis  PreliminaryWork
jcchurch@dataanalysis:~/Code$ cd HaskellDataAnalysis/
jcchurch@dataanalysis:~/Code/HaskellDataAnalysis$ ls
analysis  data
jcchurch@dataanalysis:~/Code/HaskellDataAnalysis$ cp ~/Downloads/GL2015.TXT data
/
jcchurch@dataanalysis:~/Code/HaskellDataAnalysis$ ls data/
GL2015.TXT
```

I like to create a directory for my code called Code; and inside here, I have a directory called HaskellDataAnalysis. And inside HaskellDataAnalysis, I have two directories, called analysis and data. In the analysis folder, I would like to store my notebooks. In the data folder, I would like to store my datasets.

That way, I can keep a clear distinction between analysis files and data files. That means I need to move the data file, just downloaded, into my `data` folder. So, copy `GL2015.TXT` from our `Downloads` folder into our `data` folder. If I do an `ls` on my `data` folder, I'll see that I've got my file. Now, I'm going to go into my `analysis` folder, which currently contains nothing, and I'm going to start the Jupyter Notebook as follows:

```
jcchurch@dataanalysis:~/Code/HaskellDataAnalysis$ cd analysis/
jcchurch@dataanalysis:~/Code/HaskellDataAnalysis/analysis$ ls
jcchurch@dataanalysis:~/Code/HaskellDataAnalysis/analysis$ jupyter notebook
/usr/local/lib/python3.4/dist-packages/widgetsnbextension/__init__.py:30: UserWa
rning: To use the jupyter-js-widgets nbextension, you'll need to update
    the Jupyter notebook to version 4.2 or later.
  the Jupyter notebook to version 4.2 or later.""")
[I 15:51:06.048 NotebookApp] Serving notebooks from local directory: /home/jcchu
rch/Code/HaskellDataAnalysis/analysis
[I 15:51:06.052 NotebookApp] 0 active kernels
[I 15:51:06.053 NotebookApp] The Jupyter Notebook is running at: http://localhos
t:8888/
[I 15:51:06.053 NotebookApp] Use Control-C to stop this server and shut down all
 kernels (twice to skip confirmation).
```

Type in `jupyter notebook`, which will start a web server on your computer. You can use your web browser in order to interact with Haskell:

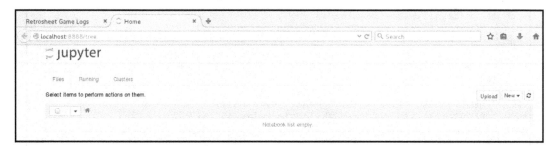

The address for the Jupyter Notebook is the localhost, on port `8888`. Now I'm going to create a new Haskell notebook. To do this, I click on the **New** drop-down button on the right side of the screen, and I find **Haskell**:

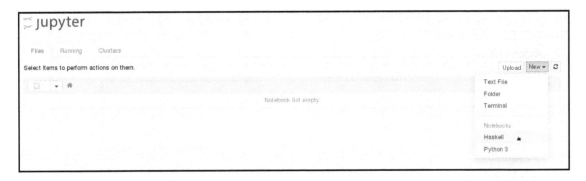

Let's begin by renaming our notebook **Baseball**, because we're going to be looking at baseball statistics:

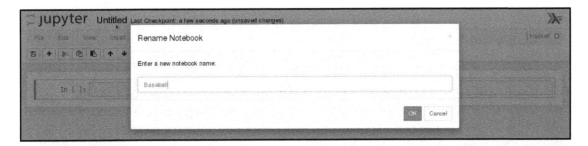

I need to import the `Text.CSV` file that we just installed. Now, if your cursor is sitting in a text field and you hit *Enter*, you'll just be making that text field larger, as shown in the following screenshot. Instead, in order to submit expressions to the Jupyter environment, you have to hit hit *Shift + Enter* on the keyboard:

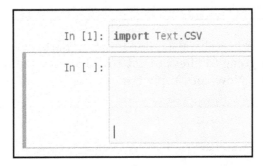

So, now that we've imported `Text.CSV`, let's create our Baseball dataset and parse the dataset. The command for this is `parseCSVFromFile`, after which we pass in the location of our text file:

```
In [2]:  baseball <- parseCSVFromFile "../data/GL2015.TXT"

In [ ]:
```

Great. If you didn't get a **File Not Found** error at this point, then that means you have successfully parsed the data from the CSV file. Now, let's explore the type of baseball data. To do this, we enter `type` and `baseball`, which is what we just created, and we see that we have either a parsing error or a CSV file:

```
In [3]:  :type baseball
              baseball :: Either ParseError CSV
```

I've already done this, so I know that there aren't any parsing errors in our CSV file, but if there were, they would be represented by `ParseError`. So I can promise you that if you've gotten this far, you know that we have a working CSV file. Now, I'll be honest: I don't know why the CSV library does this, but the last element in every CSV data is a single empty list, and I call this empty list the "empty row". What I would like to do is to create a quick function, called `noEmptyRows`, that removes any row of data that doesn't have at least two pieces of information in it:

```
In [4]:  noEmptyRows = either (const []) (filter (\row -> 2 <= length row))
```

So, if we have a parsing error, we're just going to return back an empty list, and if we actually have data, we're going to filter out any row that does not have at least two pieces of information in that row. Now, let's apply our `noEmptyRows` to our Baseball dataset:

```
In [5]:  baseballList = noEmptyRows baseball

In [6]:  length baseballList
         2429
```

I'm going to call this `baseballList`. Then we can do a quick check to see the length of the `baseballList`, and we should have 2,429 rows representing 2,429 games played in the 2015 season.

Now let's look at the type of `baseballList`, and we see that we have a list of fields:

```
In [7]: :type baseballList
        baseballList :: [[Field]]
```

Now, you may be asking yourself: What's a field? We can explore a field using `info`, and doing so will bring up a window from the bottom of the screen:

```
In [8]: :info Field

In [ ]: |


type Field = String      -- Defined in `Text.CSV'
```

It says `type Field = String`, and it's defined in this `Text.CSV` library. So, just remember that a field is just a string.

Now, because every value is a field that is also a string, that means that if I do math on strings, it's going to produce an error message, as shown in the following screenshot:

```
In [9]: "1" + 1
        No instance for (Num String) arising from a use of `+'
        Possible fix: add an instance declaration for (Num String)
        In the expression: "1" + 1
        In an equation for `it': it = "1" + 1
```

So what I need to do is to parse that information from a string to something else that I can use, such as an int or a double, and I do that with the `read` command. Let's look at an example:

```
In [10]: read "1" :: Integer
         1

In [11]: read "1.5" :: Double
         1.5
```

So if I say read "1", it will be parsed as an Integer, or, if I say read "1.5", then it will be parsed as a Double.

So, armed with this knowledge of parsing data from strings, we can parse a whole column of data. Create a readIndex function, and let's say that, in our case, each value is a cell:

```
In [12]:  readIndex :: Read cell => Either a CSV -> Int -> [cell]
          readIndex csv index = map (read . (!! index)) (noEmptyRows csv)
```

So for each cell in our dataset, we're going to pass in our original Baseball dataset—this is an Either; and we're going to say that we need an Int index position in our list; and we are going to return a list of cells. This requires two arguments: the csv, and the index position that we need. And we are going to map over each record, and we're going to read whatever exists at the specified index position. We also need the noEmptyRows function that we discussed earlier.

Now, if you recall earlier, I said that the away-team scores in our CSV file exist on column 10, and because Haskell is a zero-based index file, that means we need to pass in index 9 to our readIndex function:

```
In [13]:  readIndex baseball 9 :: [Integer]

          [3,0,0,1,6,0,1,6,5,2,3,2,10,8,3,3,2,6,6,7,12,5,0,2,5,3,0,5,0,5,0,4,4,2,5,2,1,1,5,1,6,10,2,6,1,6,4,12,6,8,6,0,5,3,3,4,1,9,
          6,1,0,6,1,4,9,8,5,2,0,3,4,9,2,0,2,2,9,10,2,8,4,8,6,7,4,7,6,8,10,4,4,6,4,8,12,6,2,2,6,5,0,4,8,2,5,3,7,4,4,2,3,8,3,5,5,2,1,
          4,5,10,2,1,1,10,7,6,0,2,1,1,2,4,2,5,4,5,7,0,2,2,1,6,4,2,3,5,8,5,3,1,3,9,1,2,4,12,0,5,4,1,9,5,6,3,4,2,1,2,5,8,1,3,2,2,10,5
          ,5,5,0,6,2,5,1,1,6,1,3,1,1,7,14,6,5,1,6,5,5,6,1,6,7,7,16,1,3,9,2,1,9,0,13,3,2,5,2,5,4,2,2,6,3,2,7,0,3,2,1,6,1,2,3,9,4,2,4
          ,2,7,2,13,1,5,0,3,4,7,4,2,3,0,3,1,4,1,8,9,8,2,2,5,0,5,5,11,5,7,3,6,4,7,4,1,8,5,2,3,4,1,5,6,5,1,3,5,4,0,6,3,3,9,4,11,11,2,
          2,2,2,5,13,2,2,2,3,14,5,2,1,5,10,3,6,5,1,13,8,8,3,3,7,2,5,2,1,2,6,5,8,3,2,3,4,3,1,0,7,3,0,0,3,0,3,2,1,0,4,11,4,2,3,7,8,6,
          4,0,1,2,4,1,2,8,7,6,6,3,7,0,5,0,6,1,6,0,2,3,5,2,7,1,5,3,0,9,4,4,0,2,7,3,2,6,0,8,2,7,0,4,2,3,5,6,11,10,0,1,5,13,5,3,1,3,9,
          6,5,3,4,4,5,3,5,0,14,2,7,1,0,9,5,4,3,2,0,6,2,7,1,8,0,2,6,10,2,7,6,6,2,2,1,6,4,3,5,6,6,1,3,2,2,2,3,2,6,1,9,2,7,3,2,4,2,5,1
          1,2,11,3,2,3,7,4,2,10,8,1,8,2,4,2,7,6,1,3,1,4,7,1,1,0,6,3,2,4,2,2,9,1,1,5,4,2,2,1,4,2,1,6,5,3,5,2,3,3,4,1,2,7,1,8,10,10,4
          ,5,7,3,10,10,6,5,5,4,4,4,10,1,11,7,5,1,5,4,4,0,2,0,11,7,0,1,3,9,0,6,1,0,10,1,1,3,2,6,4,3,1,4,3,3,8,4,0,3,5,5,4,10,8,3,0,6
          ,4,2,4,2,1,1,4,1,4,6,9,4,3,0,2,4,3,5,5,0,4,1,3,7,0,3,0,12,2,3,2,0,10,2,4,4,11,11,1,8,1,1,3,4,1,3,2,15,5,3,9,2,10,3,0,0,2,
          8,1,8,2,10,6,5,7,2,3,1,2,11,2,1,1,3,3,10,2,1,0,4,0,2,5,3,8,3,2,2,4,4,4,1,1,1,7,9,2,1,0,6,4,1,4,5,4,3,4,2,3,3,5,3,6,3,3,0,
          2,3,2,3,3,4,5,5,11,0,0,1,6,6,2,1,4,8,2,7,4,4,2,2,0,6,3,0,2,5,4,0,5,7,9,5,5,8,5,2,9,6,5,0,6,3,1,2,6,3,4,1,7,1,3,2,7,8,11,5
          ,7,4,1,6,0,5,4,2,5,2,6,3,9,2,4,2,7,0,0,7,6,3,2,6,1,2,3,9,8,6,3,4,3,5,4,8,8,7,3,6,2,1,6,7,6,2,2,3,5,4,10,7,1,2,2,10,6,6,2,
          5,5,2,7,1,4,4,2,1,2,1,4,9,5,0,7,4,4,6,7,3,0,2,3,6,6,3,0,3,4,4,6,1,3,3,5,4,3,3,2,0,2,3,0,2,1,2,8,3,5,2,3,1,5,4,2,1,9,12,7,
          5,4,2,2,1,2,4,6,8,0,5,0,0,6,6,3,0,5,4,4,3,13,0,0,5,2,5,1,4,3,0,4,1,0,0,4,5,5,8,4,7,3,1,7,5,3,1,4,2,8,5,13,1,0,1,4,1,4,4,8
          ,0,4,4,7,0,4,0,3,1,1,1,8,3,0,9,5,2,1,3,4,5,5,16,2,6,2,7,2,0,6,2,2,3,17,2,1,1,2,0,0,2,2,4,8,5,6,5,3,3,2,1,4,3,7,1,7,5,8,0,
          1,5,2,4,7,2,2,12,2,4,2,1,0,9,9,12,1,2,4,4,4,3,1,3,5,8,4,5,1,6,10,0,2,0,13,8,12,2,6,13,2,0,2,4,2,2,2,3,8,2,11,4,8,2,13,6,7
          ,6,11,0,3,8,0,5,4,2,6,3,1,1,1,2,1,2,8,1,8,5,8,6,1,5,0,1,8,8,0,0,6,4,4,5,2,5,8,0,3,3,4,3,5,4,2,7,4,1,5,2,2,8,2,2,9,3,1,4,2,5
```

Here, we parse this list that's returned as a list of integers, and we are returned a listing of every single away-team score in Major League Baseball. The very first element in our list is a 3, because that is the first record of the file.

In this section, you learned about the structure of a CSV file, how to install the Text.CSV library, and how to pull a little bit of information out of that CSV file using the CSV library. In the next section, we're going to discuss how to create our own module for descriptive statistics, and how to write a function for the range of a dataset.

Data range

We begin with the data range descriptive statistic. This will be the easiest descriptive statistic that we cover in this chapter. This is basically grabbing the maximum and minimum of a range of values. So, in this section, we're going to be taking a look at using the maximum and minimum functions in order to find the range of a dataset, and we're going to be combining those functions into a single function that returns a tuple of values. And finally, we're going to compute the range of our away-team runs using the function that we prototyped previously.

Let's go to our Haskell notebook in the Jupyter environment. In the last section, we pulled a listing of all the away-team scores for each game in the 2015 season of Major League Baseball. If you're rejoining this section after a break, you may have to find the **Kernel** and **Restart & Run All** feature inside the Notebook system:

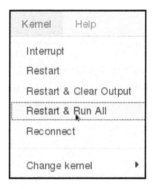

Now we get a warning message, saying that this will clear all of our variables, but that's okay because all of the variables are going to be rebuilt by the notebook.

The last thing we did was pass in index 9 to get the away scores. Now, let's store this in a variable called `awayRuns`:

```
In [14]:  awayRuns = readIndex baseball 9 :: [Integer]
```

In order to find the range of this dataset, we're going to utilize two functions, `maximum awayRuns` and `minimum awayRuns`:

```
In [15]: maximum awayRuns
         21

In [16]: minimum awayRuns
         0
```

We see that the maximum number of runs scored by any away team in the 2015 season was **21**, and we see that the minimum was **0**. Let's take a moment to examine the type signatures of the maximum and minimum functions:

```
In [17]: :type (minimum, maximum)
         (minimum, maximum) :: forall a a1. (Ord a, Ord a1) => ([a] -> a, [a1] -> a1)
```

They both take a list of values and return a single value, and the values are bound by the `Ord` type. With that knowledge, we're going to create a function, called `range`, that takes a value and returns a tuple of values bound by the `Ord` type. Let's go. Our quick function should probably look like this:

```
In [18]: range :: Ord a => [a] -> (a, a)
         range xs = (minimum xs, maximum xs)
```

So, we've called this a range, and we have bound our values by the `Ord` type. We have also accepted a range of values, and returned our tuple of values. And then, we entered `range xs`, which will extend from `minimum xs` to `maximum xs`. Now, let's test this function.

Testing `range awayRuns`, we see that we get a range of **0** to **21**:

```
In [19]: range awayRuns
         (0,21)
```

Now, what if we pass an empty list, or what if we just passed a list of one value? These are some things that we didn't consider in this function that I just wrote, so let's explore that briefly:

```
In [20]:  range []

          Prelude.minimum: empty list
```

We see that we get an error message—`Prelude.minimum: empty list`—and that's because our data was passed to the minimum function. It saw that we had an empty list and it threw an error. What we really ought to do is to package our return in a `Maybe` so that we could potentially return nothing, and adjust this for cases where we have empty list:

```
In [21]:  range :: Ord a => [a] -> Maybe (a, a)
          range [] = Nothing
          range [x] = Just (x, x)
          range xs = Just (minimum xs, maximum xs)
```

The preceding screenshot shows our improved range function. We use a little bit of pattern matching in order to adjust to some of the conditions that we should be looking for in a proper range function. So, we still have a list of values that are bound by the `Ord` type, but now, we are packaging our return inside of a `Maybe`. That way, we can adjust the circumstances in which an empty list is passed, such as by returning nothing. If we have a single value, we can just return that value twice, and not even have to worry with the minimum and maximum. But if we get anything else, we can utilize our minimum and maximum functions. This means that we can produce the range of an empty list (`range []`), `range [1]`, and our full `range awayRuns`:

```
In [22]:  range []

          Nothing

In [23]:  range [1]

          Just (1,1)

In [24]:  range awayRuns

          Just (0,21)
```

Great. So, this improved function is going to be our prototype for the remaining descriptive statistics in this book. We're going to be adjusting accordingly based on the inputs given, and returning `Nothing` in cases where no results should be given. In the next section, we're going to be discussing how to compute the mean of a dataset.

Data mean and standard deviation

The next descriptive statistics covered will be the mean, also called the average, and standard deviation. In this section, we will use the sum and length functions to compose the mean of a dataset. We'll also explore the sum and length functions; compose our mean function; and then use that mean function in order to compose a standard deviation function. Finally, we're going to compute the mean and standard deviation of the 2015 away-team runs using our function.

The mean is a summary statistic that gives you a rough idea of the middle values of the dataset, while not truly being the middle of a dataset:

$$mean(X) = \bar{X} = \frac{1}{n} \sum_{i=1}^{n} X_i$$

The mean is trivial to calculate and thus it is frequently used, and it is the sum of that dataset divided by the number of values in that dataset.

We will also discuss sample standard deviation, which is the mean distance from the mean and a measure of a dataset spread. The approach that we will be using is known as the sample standard deviation. I have presented the function here for your reference:

$$\sigma = \sqrt{\frac{1}{n-1} \sum_{i=1}^{n} (X_i - \bar{X})^2}$$

Now, let's go over to our Linux environment. We left off last section discussing the range of a dataset. Let's add a new import now, `Data.Maybe`, as follows:

```
In [25]:  import Text.CSV
          import Data.Maybe
```

Here, we have added a library. Each time we add libraries, we will restart and rerun all, and it's okay to do this. It will take a moment, and will reload all of our variables.

In order to compute the mean of a dataset, we add up all the values and divide this value by the length of those values. So, in order to find the sum of all the values in a list, we use sum on the awayRuns variable, and we also need to find the length of the awayRuns variable:

```
In [25]:  sum awayRuns

          10091

In [26]:  length awayRuns

          2429
```

There were 10,091 runs scored in the 2015 season by the away team, and 2,429 games played in that season. We divide the first number by the second, and we get our average; but we need to explore the type of the sum and the length functions:

```
In [27]:  :type sum

          sum :: forall a. Num a => [a] -> a

In [28]:  :type length

          length :: forall a. [a] -> Int
```

We can see that the sum takes a list of values and returns a value, and the sum inputs and the outputs are bound by the Num type, whereas the inputs on length aren't bound by anything, and they always return an int. The division operator in Haskell doesn't work with int, so what we need to do is to convert the values returned by sum and length to something that we can work with:

```
In [29]:  realToFrac (sum awayRuns) / fromIntegral (length awayRuns)

          4.154384520378756
```

So the function we have used for this is `realToFrac`, where we pass sum of the away runs divided by `fromIntegral`, which takes the length of the away runs. So, our average is **4.15** runs per game scored by away teams in the 2015 season. We use this information in order to compose our mean function:

```
In [30]:  mean :: Real a => [a] -> Maybe Double
          mean []  = Nothing
          mean [x] = Just $ realToFrac x
          mean xs  = Just $ realToFrac (sum xs) / fromIntegral (length xs)
```

Much like our range function, we have a return type of a double that's been packaged into a `Maybe`, and we have a list of values that are bound on the `Real` type. Our function uses pattern matching in order to handle the variety of inputs and outputs that we will likely receive, much like we did with the range function in the last section. So, if we have a list of no values, we return **Nothing**. Now, it's best that we return **Nothing**, and not 0, because 0 could be interpreted as a mean of a dataset. If we have a single value, then we're just going to return that value bundled in `Just`, and if we have a list, then we're actually going to implement the sum and length functions that we described earlier. So, let's test this out:

```
In [31]:  mean []

          Nothing

In [32]:  mean [1]

          Just 1.0

In [33]:  mean awayRuns

          Just 4.154384520378756
```

As we can see, if we get the mean of an empty list, we should get `Nothing`; if we get mean of a single value, we should get that value converted to a double; and if we have mean of a true list, we should get our average, which in our case is **4.15**.

Now, any function that uses our mean function is going to have to interpret the value inside of `Maybe`, so in order to do that, we use a function called `fromJust`. Now, let's write the code for the standard deviation, as follows:

```
In [34]:   stdev :: Real a => [a] -> Maybe Double
           stdev []  = Nothing
           stdev [_] = Nothing
           stdev xs = Just $ sqrt (sumsquares / n_m1)
             where
               n_m1 = fromIntegral (length xs - 1)
               meanxs = fromJust (mean xs)
               sumsquares = sum $ map (diffsquare . realToFrac) xs
               diffsquare x = (x - meanxs) * (x - meanxs)
```

Much like the mean function we wrote earlier, we have our inputs bound by a `Real` type; and we will be returning a Double packaged to the Maybe. And for historical reasons, we will call this function `stdev`. Statistical spreadsheet software and statistical packages will call this particular function `stdev`, which is a recreation of the formula that we saw at the beginning of this section, which produces the sample standard deviation. It's important to note that the sample standard deviation requires at least two values in order to compute a spread. You can't very well compute a spread with one value, and so we need to use pattern matching in order to detect that, thus if we have an empty list, we return `Nothing`. If we have a list of just one item, we still return `Nothing`. After that, we have actually implemented the formula necessary for the sample standard deviation. Let's do a few tests:

```
In [35]:  stdev []

          Nothing

In [36]:  stdev [1]

          Nothing

In [37]:  stdev awayRuns

          Just 3.1155073817635124
```

So, the standard deviation of a blank list is `Nothing`; the standard deviation of a single item is still `Nothing`; and the standard deviation of our `awayRuns` is `3.12`. With this information, we are going to take our average which is `4.15`, and we will subtract it with `3.12` and we will also add `3.12` to it:

```
In [38]:  (4.15 - 3.12, 4.15 + 3.12)

          (1.0300000000000002,7.2700000000000005)
```

We can say that one standard deviation range of our away-team runs for the 2015 season is **1.03** runs to **7.27** runs; and that gives us a good idea of where the majority of the scores were for away teams in the 2015 season. So, in this section, we looked at the mean and the standard deviations of a dataset. We implemented the functions; we discussed the sum and the length functions necessary for those functions; and then we did a few examples of how we could find the mean and standard deviation with the functions that we had prototyped. In the next section, we will be discussing the median of a dataset.

Data median

The median of a dataset is the true middle value of the values sorted. Now, if there isn't a single middle value, such as if there's an even number of elements in the list, then we take the average of the two values closest to the sorted middle. In this video, we're going to discuss the algorithm for computing the median of a dataset, and we're going to take the traditional approach of sorting the values first and then selecting the values we need in order to compute the median. We're going to be testing the circumstances under which the median function should behave, and then we're going to compute the median of our 2015 away-team runs using our prototyped function.

In the last section, we were discussing the mean and standard deviation of runs; and we found that one standard deviation range was 1.03 to 7.27. Now, for this topic, we will have to add yet another import, and we're going to import `Data.List`, as this is where we find the sort function:

```
In [*]:  import Text.CSV
         import Data.Maybe
         import Data.List
```

Now, as usual, we will restart and rerun all so that everything is properly loaded for our notebook. Next, let's create a couple of quick lists, just to demonstrate the `sort` function:

```
In [39]:  oddList = [3,4,1,2,5]

In [40]:  evenList = [6,5,4,3,2,1]
```

So, here we have `oddList`, which contains the comma-separated values "3,4,1,2,5", and we have an `evenList`, which contains "6,5,4,3,2,1". We can use the `sort` function to sort these lists as follows:

```
In [41]: sort oddList
         [1,2,3,4,5]

In [42]: sort evenList
         [1,2,3,4,5,6]
```

This was pretty straightforward—the `sort` function is found in the `Data.List` library. If we wish to find the middle value of a list, we need to find the length of the list and then divide by **2**:

```
In [43]: length oddList `div` 2
         2
```

So, we have used the length of `oddList` and then divided it by 2, and it produces **2**. Now we can sort that odd list and pull out the second element:

```
In [44]: sort oddList !! 2
         3
```

After sorting, we got **3**; and **3** is the median of our odd list. And for an odd list, that's all you have to do.

Whenever we pass an even list, you should notice that we get the index position that appears after the median. So, if we divide the length of `evenList` by 2, we will get 3 as shown in the following screenshot:

```
In [45]: length evenList `div` 2
         3
```

The index position for **3** in our sorted even list will be **4**, which is not the median. So, we need to take the two values that are closest to the middle, which in this case it will be index **3**; and then the index position before that, which is **2**; and then add those together and divide by **2**. So, the formula is as follows:

```
In [46]:  ((sort evenList !! 3) + (sort evenList !! 2)) / 2

          3.5
```

As we can see that our median is 3.5, which is the true median of our even list. There are algorithms for finding the median that do not require the full sort of values, such as you can use the `quickselect` algorithm to quickly find the median sorted value in a list. But for our purposes, we're going to stay with the traditional sort the values first approach. We're going to prototype a median function utilizing the approach that we've outlined here. We're going to go over a few quick examples of what should happen whenever median is called:

```
In [47]:  median :: Real a => [a] -> Maybe Double
          median [] = Nothing
          median list
          | odd (length list) = Just middleValue
          | otherwise = Just middleEven
          where
              sorted = sort list
              middleIndex = length list `div` 2
              middleValue = realToFrac $ sorted !! middleIndex
              beforeMiddleValue = realToFrac $ sorted !! (middleIndex - 1)
              middleEven = 0.5 * (middleValue + beforeMiddleValue)
```

So, here is our median prototyped function. Notice that we are bounding our inputs based on type `Real`, and we are packaging once again a `Double` inside of a Maybe. We're using Double because, you know, there's the possibility that even though we have a full list of integers, we still need to return a double because we have an even number of integers. If we have a median of no items, then we return `Nothing`. Other than that, we are going to have the possibility of an odd list; then we will return the `middleValue`. Otherwise, we are going to return the `middleEven`. After that, we have outlined all of the different circumstances. So, let's test out a few examples:

Whenever we return the median of an empty list, we get Nothing. Likewise, if we get the median of oddList, we should get back **3**. Notice it's been converted to a double. And if we do the median of an evenList, we get **3.5**. And to outline again, we have our middleValue, which is just the middleIndex; and we have the beforeMiddleValue, which is middleIndex – 1. And the middleEven is simply those two values divided by 2; and that's all there really is to it. We're using the odd function in order to look for an odd number of elements; otherwise, we're going to use the even approach.

So, using sort, we built a function for finding the median of a list. This was a long function, and we described it in detail. Finally, we need to use the median function, which we have prototyped already, in order to find the away runs:

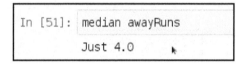

We found that the middle sorted value of array runs in the 2015 season is 4. In our next section, we are going to discuss what's probably the simplest of the descriptive statistics to discuss, and that is the mode, but it turns out to be one of the more difficult to compute.

Data mode

The mode is the value in a list which appears the most frequently. In this section, we are going to discuss an algorithm for finding the mode. We will first try to understand how the mode of a list can be solved using **Run-Length Encoding** (**RLE**). We will then break that problem of RLE into parts, and then write the code for our function. Finally, we will use RLE in order to find the mode of a dataset, and then we're going to compute the mode of our 2015 away runs dataset.

To find the mode, we will have to do yet another import. We need to go back up to the very top of the Baseball dataset and import `Data.Ord`:

```
In [1]:  import Text.CSV
         import Data.Maybe
         import Data.List
         import Data.Ord
```

We need this for a function that we'll use later on in this section. Now, let's restart and rerun all—it'll take a moment. Next, let's create a list, called `myList`, that we will use in order to demonstrate the mode:

```
In [52]:  myList = [4,4,5,5,4]
```

Now the value that appears the most frequently in this list, of course, is 4. Next, we would like to introduce an algorithm known as RLE. Now, RLE is an algorithm for lossless compression and it has a few interesting applications to it. We can find the mode of a list by first running RLE, and in order to find RLE, we need to understand how elements group together. So, there is a function in `Data.List`, called `group`, which can help create a list of list, and each sublist in our primary list is a grouping of the values as follows:

```
In [53]:  group myList
          [[4,4],[5,5],[4]]
```

So, here we have `group List [[4,4], [5,5], [4]]`. Now we can easily count each element in the sublist, thus creating a run-length encoding. So, let's create a function to represent RLE, which we need to be of the right type for our values:

```
In [54]:  runLengthEncoding :: Ord a => [a] -> [(a, Integer)]
          runLengthEncoding = (map (\xs -> (head xs, genericLength xs)) . group)
```

We're going to accept any element as an input, and then return a list consisting of a tuple of those elements, followed by an integer, where the integer is going to represent the number of sub-elements in that list. So, `runLengthEncoding` is going to be any list we get in, and we are going to map over that list. With that sublist, we will first get the head of the list; and second, we will get the generic length of `xs`. Once we get that generic length, we're going to compute the group:

```
In [55]:  runLengthEncoding myList
              [(4,2),(5,2),(4,1)]
```

So, if we pass in `runLengthEncoding` of our `myList`, we compute the run-length encoding of our original list, where each element in order represents the element that is seen and how many times that element is seen. We got `[(4,2), (5,2), (4,1)]`, so there'll be an even number of elements; and for convenience's sake, we group them in tuples.

If we do `runLengthEncoding` with an empty list, we will get back an empty list:

```
In [56]:  runLengthEncoding []
              []
```

But here's where it gets interesting. If we do `runLengthEncoding` and we first sort `myList` of values, we now have a tuple of values where all of the 4s are grouped together and all of the 5s are grouped together:

```
In [57]:  runLengthEncoding (sort myList)
              [(4,3),(5,2)]
```

So, we have three 4s and two 5s. Now what we can do is perform run-length encoding on the sorted version of our dataset, and then look for whatever tuple has the highest second value. So, this next algorithm computes the mode of a list using the `runLengthEncoding` function, and here, we are using a function called `maximumBy`:

```
In [58]:  mode :: Ord a => [a] -> Maybe (a, Integer)
          mode [] = Nothing
          mode list = Just $ maximumBy (comparing snd) pairs
            where
                sorted = sort list
                pairs = runLengthEncoding sorted
```

maximumBy is found in the Data.Ord library, and it requires that we are comparing based on whatever the second value is, that is, the snd; and we are comparing on whatever that integer is, which, as we identified earlier, is the length of a sublist. All our mode function does is sorts the values, passes that data to runLengthEncoding, and then finds which element in the list has the highest second value, thus representing the mode. Let's check this out:

```
In [59]: mode []
         Nothing

In [60]: mode myList
         Just (4,3)
```

So, if we pass in an empty list to our mode, we get back Nothing, and if we pass myList to the mode from our earlier example, we get back Just 4, 3. So, the first element in the tuple will be the most frequently seen element, and the second element is how many times that first element is seen. In our case, 4 is seen 3 times. We've been working with our Baseball dataset, and we have our away-team runs, so now we can find which away-team run appears most frequently in the 2015 baseball season:

```
In [61]: mode awayRuns
         Just (2,379)
```

mode awayRuns will give us the answer that there were 379 games in the season in which 2 runs were scored, and that 2 runs was the most frequently seen result.

Summary

In this chapter, we recalled data stored in a CSV file using the Text.CSV library, and we implemented the descriptive statistic functions for the range, mean, median, mode, and standard deviation. These functions will become our DescriptiveStats module for future sections. In our next chapter, we will begin using SQLite3.

2
SQLite3

In this chapter, we are going to learn about SQLite3. SQLite3 is a file format for storing data in the same mindset of a relational database such as Oracle, MySQL, MariaDB, and Postgres. Well, I suppose that you could use SQLite3 as a traditional database engine, but it's really not made for that. SQLite3 allows us to open up a file, work with the data in that file using SQL statements, and then close that file. One file can contain one database, and a database can store multiple tables of information. Contrast this with the CSV file format that we used in the last chapter which, at best, stores a single table of information. The advantages of SQLite3 are that it doesn't require any server-side programs running in the background, there are no configurations to discuss, and the executable for working with SQLite3 is a single file. So, in my opinion, working with data in an SQLite3 file format is more versatile than working with data in a CSV file format.

In this chapter, we'll focus on how to get our data from CSV into SQLite3. Then we'll be training ourselves to think of our dataset in terms of a database using SQL statements to fetch data, which requires an understanding of SELECT queries. We do need to craft some code for translating the output from our SELECT queries into Haskell, and we'll demonstrate how to use our data summary functions from Chapter 1, *SQLite3*, with our database.

In this chapter, we will cover the following topics:

- Importing a CSV file into an SQLite 3 table
- Understanding the data types of SQLite3 and running SELECT queries
- Creating slices of data within SQLite3 and Haskell
- Computing descriptive statistics using our SQLite3 dataset and our module

SQLite3 command line

This section is going to be a primer on SQLite3 and it won't have any Haskell code. We're going to take a moment, and translate a CSV file into SQLite3. In this section, we're going to take a look at introducing SQLite3; we will be creating a table in an SQLite3 database, and also adding a CSV file to that table that we created in our SQLite3 database.

So, let's go to our Haskell environment and open our browser. Using Google, search for `usgs earthquake feed csv`. USG is the United States Geological Survey, and they keep a database of every single earthquake that takes place on planet earth, and they offer this data in a CSV file. So, we're going to click that very first link, `https://earthquake.usgs.gov/earthquakes/feed/v1.0/csv.php`. You should see **Spreadsheet Format** at the top; scroll down to the heading where it says **Past 7 Days** on the right side of the page, and we want to find **All earthquakes**. We will have the option to download the `all_week.csv` file for all earthquakes that have happened in the past seven days in the United States:

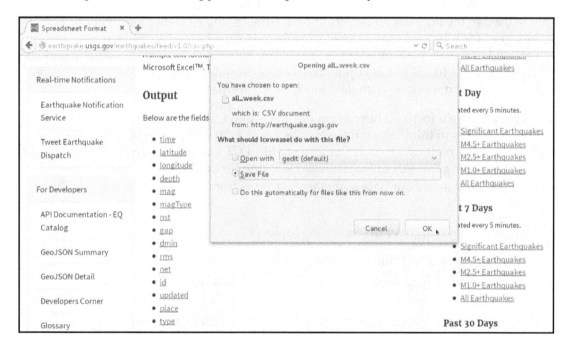

So, let's save that file and go over to our Terminal, and type in `ls`:

```
File  Edit  View  Search  Terminal  Help
jcchurch@dataanalysis:~/Downloads$ ls
all_week.csv  GL2015.TXT  gl2015.zip
jcchurch@dataanalysis:~/Downloads$ ▊
```

We see that we have, in our `Downloads` folder, an `all_week` CSV file; that's the file that we just downloaded. Let's convert this file to a CSV file by using the command shown in the following screenshot:

```
File  Edit  View  Search  Terminal  Help
jcchurch@dataanalysis:~/Downloads$ ls
all_week.csv  GL2015.TXT  gl2015.zip
jcchurch@dataanalysis:~/Downloads$ vi all_week.csv ▊
```

Now, let's take a look at the file. You can see that this particular file has a header line, and we can look at the header information of all of our columns:

```
File  Edit  View  Search  Terminal  Help
time,latitude,longitude,depth,mag,magType,nst,gap,dmin,rms,net,id,updated,place,
type,horizontalError,depthError,magError,magNst,status,locationSource,magSource
2016-07-11T19:44:16.470Z,38.2513,-115.9473,20.2,1.7,ml,11,176.49,1.034,,nn,nn005
51404,2016-07-11T19:46:20.977Z,"37km E of Warm Springs, Nevada",earthquake,,,,,a
utomatic,nn,nn
2016-07-11T19:38:52.140Z,38.2467,-118.6373,7,0.8,ml,6,200.49,0.095,,nn,nn0055140
3,2016-07-11T19:41:07.909Z,"30km S of Hawthorne, Nevada",earthquake,,,,,automati
c,nn,nn
2016-07-11T19:27:19.750Z,38.6712,-117.0597,0.3,1.7,ml,9,159.2,0.888,,nn,nn005514
02,2016-07-11T19:29:35.169Z,"68km NNE of Tonopah, Nevada",earthquake,,,,,automat
ic,nn,nn
2016-07-11T19:01:47.820Z,48.0008333,-121.9131667,11.92,1.8,ml,12,93,0.2198,0.18,
uw,uw61179846,2016-07-11T19:15:53.980Z,"9km NE of Three Lakes, Washington",earth
quake,0.44,2.69,0.107,20,reviewed,uw,uw
2016-07-11T18:48:12.000Z,60.2407,-141.6943,13.7,1.3,ml,,,,0.49,ak,ak13751113,201
6-07-11T19:07:17.191Z,"45km ENE of Cape Yakataga, Alaska",earthquake,0.2,0.1,,,a
utomatic,ak,ak
2016-07-11T18:46:07.360Z,33.695,-117.4286667,5.76,1.14,ml,29,86,0.04586,0.2,ci,c
i37412463,2016-07-11T18:49:57.670Z,"10km WNW of Lake Elsinore, CA",earthquake,0.
33,0.79,0.165,29,automatic,ci,ci
2016-07-11T18:44:07.370Z,47.166,-121.9456667,-1.06,0.94,ml,8,121,0.03681,0.18,uw
,uw61179836,2016-07-11T19:11:40.350Z,"5km SE of Enumclaw, Washington",explosion,
0.68,31.61,0.049,5,reviewed,uw,uw
"all_week.csv" 1586 lines, 293297 characters
```

The first five pieces of information on every record will be the time, latitude, longitude, depth, and magnitude. There's a lot of other information here that we could go through but for our purposes, we just want those first five columns of information. What we can do in order to narrow this dataset down to just those first five columns of information is to use a command called `cut`. `cut` is a very useful command for working with CSV files and we have to pass it a delimiter; the delimiter is going to be a comma because this is a comma-separated value file and we need to know what fields we would like to keep from our file. As we want the first five columns, we will type in the following command:

```
jcchurch@dataanalysis:~/Downloads$ cut -d, -f 1,2,3,4,5 all_week.csv > earthquak
es.csv
jcchurch@dataanalysis:~/Downloads$
```

So, we type in `1,2,3,4,5` and we separate them all through commas, then we will pass in our filename, and we are going to name this as `earthquakes.csv`. Now that file, as you recall, had a header line; and we need to chop that header line out of the file. So, there is another tool that we could use in Linux, and it's called `tail`. If we type in `tail -n +2 earthquakes.csv`, we are then going to create a temporary file:

```
jcchurch@dataanalysis:~/Downloads$ tail -n +2 earthquakes.csv > e.tmp
jcchurch@dataanalysis:~/Downloads$
```

The `e.tmp` file is our temporary file, which will be our original file of `earthquakes.csv` but without that header line. Now, we can move our temp file over our earthquakes file, and this is the primed dataset that we would like to use. Here is the command:

```
jcchurch@dataanalysis:~/Downloads$ mv e.tmp earthquakes.csv
jcchurch@dataanalysis:~/Downloads$
```

So, let's take a look at `earthquakes.csv`:

```
jcchurch@dataanalysis:~/Downloads$ vi earthquakes.csv
```

The following screenshot shows all of the earthquake data over the past seven days:

```
File  Edit  View  Search  Terminal  Help
2016-07-11T19:44:16.470Z,38.2513,-115.9473,20.2,1.7
2016-07-11T19:38:52.140Z,38.2467,-118.6373,7,0.8
2016-07-11T19:27:19.750Z,38.6712,-117.0597,0.3,1.7
2016-07-11T19:01:47.820Z,48.0008333,-121.9131667,11.92,1.8
2016-07-11T18:48:12.000Z,60.2407,-141.6943,13.7,1.3
2016-07-11T18:46:07.360Z,33.695,-117.4286667,5.76,1.14
2016-07-11T18:44:07.370Z,47.166,-121.9456667,-1.06,0.94
2016-07-11T18:41:17.000Z,60.6685,-152.2512,95.3,1.2
2016-07-11T18:29:45.000Z,61.2845,-152.5106,0,2.5
2016-07-11T18:02:27.000Z,61.4573,-149.846,52.5,1.3
2016-07-11T17:55:48.650Z,40.4318333,-121.4878333,3.94,1.45
2016-07-11T17:49:03.850Z,40.433,-121.4865,4.13,0.41
2016-07-11T17:42:43.550Z,47.2966667,-122.3013333,16.36,1.67
2016-07-11T17:23:52.610Z,40.4321667,-121.4848333,3.85,0.39
2016-07-11T17:22:30.970Z,49.015,-122.1351667,-0.87,0.79
2016-07-11T17:07:44.040Z,46.5736667,-121.7175,0.25,1.2
2016-07-11T16:59:27.140Z,40.4268333,-121.4921667,2.93,2.07
2016-07-11T16:59:11.110Z,40.4315,-121.488,3.88,0.25
2016-07-11T16:56:00.790Z,33.365,-116.7905,11.82,0.47
2016-07-11T16:54:45.260Z,36.7864,142.1313,29.75,4.7
2016-07-11T16:51:07.420Z,34.0193333,-117.1201667,1.16,1.86
2016-07-11T16:30:08.730Z,45.8876667,-122.439,-0.97,1.23
2016-07-11T16:29:32.450Z,40.432,-121.487,4.13,1.15
"earthquakes.csv" 1585 lines, 84915 characters
```

We can see that there are 1,585 earthquakes represented in this dataset and we have the first five columns of information, which is the time, latitude, longitude, depth, and magnitude. Next, we need to install SQLite3 and the SQLite3 development library; and in Debian, the command for this is as follows:

```
sudo apt-get install sqlite3 libsqlite3-dev
```

Now that SQLite3 is installed on our system, we want to create our first SQLite3 database. Typically, SQLite3 database files end with the `.sqlite3` extension. Since this is a database from the US Geological Survey, we are going to call our database using the following command:

```
sqlite3 usgs.sqlite3
```

That just created the database file on our hard drive. There's nothing in that file. There are no tables. What we need to do next is to create that first table. We're going to create a table called `earthquakes`, and then we are going to pass in the five columns from our file:

```
sqlite> CREATE TABLE earthquakes (time TEXT, latitude FLOAT, longitude FLOAT, de
pth FLOAT, magnitude FLOAT);
```

We are going to name them `time`, `latitude`, `longitude`, `depth`, and `magnitude`. Now, the first field is going to be of type `Text`, and so we have put the word `TEXT` after time; but the remaining four fields are all going to be based on floating-point numbers, and so we have used `FLOAT` type for those four types. Now, this has created the table in our `usgs.sqlite3` database file, but it doesn't have any of the information in that table. What we would like to do is to import our data from CSV into SQLite3:

```
sqlite> .mode csv
sqlite> .import earthquakes.csv earthquakes
```

We need to tell SQLite3 in order to read from CSV, and the command for that is `.mode csv`. Next up, we perform the actual import as seen in the preceding screenshot, and then we need to tell it the name of the table; we named our table `earthquakes`.

If you didn't get any error messages, this means that you have created and imported all of the data from our Past 7 Days USGS earthquake feed into an SQLite3 database. Now, let's run run a simple `SELECT` query:

```
sqlite> SELECT * FROM earthquakes LIMIT 5;
2016-07-11T19:44:16.470Z,38.2513,-115.9473,20.2,1.7
2016-07-11T19:38:52.140Z,38.2467,-118.6373,7.0,0.8
2016-07-11T19:27:19.750Z,38.6712,-117.0597,0.3,1.7
2016-07-11T19:01:47.820Z,48.0008333,-121.9131667,11.92,1.8
2016-07-11T18:48:12.000Z,60.2407,-141.6943,13.7,1.3
sqlite>
```

So, here we see `SELECT * FROM earthquakes LIMIT 5;`, and what this means is we want five records from our database, but we really don't care which records they are and give us all columns from those records. So, we got the result as shown in the preceding screenshot. Now, in order to get out of this interface, we hit *Ctrl + D* on the keyboard. If you've gotten this far, you should see a new file on your folder called `usgs.sqlite3`:

```
jcchurch@dataanalysis:~/Downloads$ ls -al
total 3552
drwxr-xr-x  2 jcchurch jcchurch    4096 Jul 11 14:58 .
drwxr-xr-x 31 jcchurch jcchurch    4096 Jul 11 14:59 ..
-rw-r--r--  1 jcchurch jcchurch  293297 Jul 11 14:53 all_week.csv
-rw-r--r--  1 jcchurch jcchurch   84915 Jul 11 14:55 earthquakes.csv
-rw-r--r--  1 jcchurch jcchurch 2648768 Dec 30  2015 GL2015.TXT
-rw-r--r--  1 jcchurch jcchurch  486057 Jun 29 15:45 gl2015.zip
-rw-r--r--  1 jcchurch jcchurch  110592 Jul 11 14:58 usgs.sqlite3
jcchurch@dataanalysis:~/Downloads$ 
```

`usgs.sqlite3` will have a little bit of information in it. If it's not the exact same size as mine, don't worry. There's going to be a different number of earthquakes going around the earth, depending on when you read this chapter. So, your size of the file will more than likely be different from mine, but you should have a few thousand earthquakes in that database.

Now, let's pretend that we're working with multiple CSV files. We can repeat our steps in this section and create a table in our SQLite3 database for each CSV file, and then import each CSV file into that database. This allows us to package many tables of information into a single file that can be represented with a clean, consistent interface. So, SQLite3 has lots of advantages, but it's not enough. We need a language like Haskell for serious number crunching. In our next section, we'll be discussing how to work with SQLite3 and Haskell.

Working with SQLite3 and Haskell

In this section, we will talk about getting data from SQLite3 into Haskell. We're going to understand the basic types within SQLite3 and their Haskell counterparts. We're also going to be installing the necessary software in order to get Haskell and SQLite3 to communicate with each other, and we're going to be writing a few SELECT queries within Haskell.

There are a few different data types in SQLite3 with their Haskell counterparts:

SQLite3	Haskell
INTEGER	Integer
REAL	Decimal
TEXT	String
BLOB	String

The four primary types are INTEGER, REAL, TEXT, and BLOB; TEXT and BLOB are almost the same types. One is for raw data and the other is for string data, but we can interpret both of those in Haskell as String. INTEGER corresponds to Integer; REAL corresponds to Decimal. There is a fifth type in SQLite3 called NUMERIC, which is adaptive and is treated as an integer with INTEGER data and a real with REAL data. For those instances in which you have a column with both, I recommend that you don't use NUMERIC at all and you just use that REAL column heading. Now, we're going to go back to our virtual environment for running our Haskell notebooks. I have my Terminal open to the `/Code/HaskellDataAnalysis` directory, and I have two folders under my `HaskellDataAnalysis` folder: `analysis` and `data`. What we would do now is to move our database, which we created in the last section, into the `data` folder. So, let's copy, from `Downloads`, the `usgs.sqlite3` file into our `data` folder:

```
jcchurch@dataanalysis:~/Code/HaskellDataAnalysis$ cp ~/Downloads/usgs.sqlite3 da
ta/
```

What we need to do now is to install the necessary software to get Haskell and SQLite3 to communicate with each other. We need a few drivers. So, let's run the following command:

sudo apt-get install libghc-hdbc-sqlite3-dev

We're going to be needing it for our next task. We also need a few libraries from Cabal, so let's get them as well:

cabal install HDBC and HDBC_sqlite3.

It will take some time to install, and it's going to download and install those libraries into our `home` folder. We're ready. So, let's start our Jupyter Notebook by typing `jupyter notebook` in our Terminal.

In the browser, inside our `analysis` folder, we are going to create a new Haskell notebook, and this will be renamed `Earthquakes`. Let's go ahead and import our database tools. Here are the following tools that we will need:

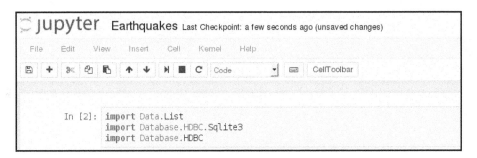

Alright, with that, we should be able to connect to our SQLite3 database. Now hopefully, you have put your data in your SQLite3 database into the `data` folder, as we did before turning on our notebook. Let's create a connection to our database. So, the command for creating a connection to the database is as follows:

```
In [3]:  db <- connectSqlite3 "../data/usgs.sqlite3"
```

So, we have passed in the path of our database file as a string. If you didn't get an error message, that means the connection was made and you should be ready to go. Let's issue our first query, to see if we get back any data. This will be a similar query to what we did in the last section, except we'll be doing it from the inside of Haskell:

```
In [4]:  records <- quickQuery db "SELECT * FROM earthquakes LIMIT 5" []
```

So, we have done records, and the command for a quick query is `quickQuery`. We then passed in the first argument as the database connection, `db`, and then we have passed in our SELECT statement. So, we're going to select everything from earthquakes, and we're going to limit that response to five records. We then pass in an empty list, so adding square brackets at the end is a way of passing in arguments into the SELECT query. We have got a really simple query, so we are not using it, but we still need to have that empty list there. So, that's the purpose of the empty list at the end of the `quickQuery` call. Now, let's take a look at what is returned by records:

```
In [5]:  records
         [[SqlByteString "2016-07-11T19:44:16.470Z",SqlDouble 38.2513,SqlDouble (-115.9473),SqlDouble 20.2,SqlDouble 1.7],[SqlByte
         String "2016-07-11T19:38:52.140Z",SqlDouble 38.2467,SqlDouble (-118.6373),SqlDouble 7.0,SqlDouble 0.8],[SqlByteString "20
         16-07-11T19:27:19.750Z",SqlDouble 38.6712,SqlDouble (-117.0597),SqlDouble 0.3,SqlDouble 1.7],[SqlByteString "2016-07-11T1
         9:01:47.820Z",SqlDouble 48.0008333,SqlDouble (-121.9131667),SqlDouble 11.92,SqlDouble 1.8],[SqlByteString "2016-07-11T18:
         48:12.000Z",SqlDouble 60.2407,SqlDouble (-141.6943),SqlDouble 13.7,SqlDouble 1.3]]
```

You can see that we have a list of records here. Let's make sure that we get 5, because that's how many we specified in the SQL query:

```
In [6]:  length records
         5
```

There you go, we got 5 records.

Now, similar to what we did in our first section, we're going to create a quick function using the function `fromSql` in order to parse data from a column into a more familiar Double type. So, let's create our quick function:

```
In [8]:  readColumn = map fromSql
```

We have named it `readColumn`, and also, what we have done is call `map fromSql`, and we're going to produce this partial function called `readColumn`. Now, there is another function in `Data.List` called `transpose`, and it allows us to perform essentially a matrix transpose on a two-dimensional data type, which `records` is. This allows us to pull a record as an entire row from the dataset. So, the fourth column in our dataset is the depth, and if we do a transpose, we can say *Give me the third row*, because all indices in Haskell are zero-based. Here is the command:

```
In [9]:  readColumn (transpose records !! 3) :: [Double]
         [20.2,7.0,0.3,11.92,13.7]
```

So, we have done a transpose on the fourth column, so the index is 3, and we're going to read it as `Double` type. We now have the depths of the five earthquakes in this particular dataset.

In the next section, we're going to examine the essential features of the SELECT query that make it so useful. If you're already a whiz at SQL, you should be able to safely skip the next section. If SQL is unfamiliar to you, then sit tight. You're going to be learning about how to slice up data with SQL in the Haskell environment.

Slices of data

This section will be an overview of the versatility of the SELECT query in SQLite3. Most of the content of this section will pertain to the inner workings of the SELECT query, and not the Haskell language itself. We're going to have an understanding of the following SELECT clauses: WHERE, ORDER BY, and LIMIT. Each of these have their own utility, but when these clauses work together you can quickly see how data can be sliced into workable chunks that can be studied later. This is my preferred way of working with data where we let SQL do the slicing and Haskell do the dicing. Once we have a data slice that we're happy with, we'll spend some time at the end looking at how to parse that chunk of data into something usable by Haskell.

Let's go back to our Jupyter Notebook; we will flop over to our primary Earthquakes notebook. We will begin with a really simple question. If our dataset of worldwide earthquakes is truly worldwide, shouldn't there be a nearly equal number of northern hemisphere earthquakes/southern hemisphere earthquakes? Only one way to find out. An earthquake is in the northern hemisphere if it has a positive latitude, so let's start by counting the number of earthquakes that meet the criteria of having a positive latitude. We're going to call this the `northern` dataset:

```
In [10]: northern <- quickQuery db "SELECT * FROM earthquakes WHERE latitude > 0" []

In [11]: length northern
         1530
```

All right, we have `1530`. That seems like a lot. Let's do the same for earthquakes in the southern latitude. This is going to be relatively straightforward, as we're just looking for earthquakes with a negative latitude:

```
In [12]: southern <- quickQuery db "SELECT * FROM earthquakes WHERE latitude < 0" []

In [13]: length southern
         55
```

There's only `55`. So, that's nowhere close to being equal; and what could account for these differences? So, at the time of writing, I personally contacted the US Geological Survey and asked them to explain this discrepancy between over 1,000 earthquakes in the northern hemisphere and less than 100 in the southern hemisphere. The reasoning I got back was that there are simply more earthquake monitors in North America, hence there are more earthquakes recorded; and that's really all there is. Since we're on the topic of North America, let's record how many earthquakes are in the northwest hemisphere, and that will require that we look at all of the earthquakes with a positive latitude and a negative longitude. So, this is an instance where we get to use the AND Boolean operator. So, we're going to call this `northwest`:

```
In [14]: northwest <- quickQuery db "SELECT * FROM earthquakes WHERE latitude > 0 AND longitude < 0" []

In [15]: length northwest
         1477
```

So, we got 1477 northwest earthquakes. Since we know there's not going to be many earthquakes in the southwest hemisphere, let's go ahead and look at the magnitude and depth of those earthquakes. First, we are going to get the southwest earthquakes where our condition would be both latitude and longitude less than zero:

```
In [17]:  southwest <- quickQuery db "SELECT * FROM earthquakes WHERE latitude < 0 AND longitude < 0" []

In [18]:  length southwest

          28
```

So, we got only 28 southwest earthquakes. So, with the southwest dataset we are going to do what we did at the very end of the last section, where we performed the transpose to look at the depth information. Let's go ahead and run the following command:

```
In [19]:  readColumn (transpose southwest !! 3) :: [Double]
          [8.12,45.25,271.75,35.56,114.67,10.0,10.0,10.0,10.0,177.68,118.76,35.41,36.89,10.0,10.0,109.76,10.0,36.59,44.27,94.22,36.
          89,10.0,10.0,10.0,10.0,39.51,11.2,93.55]
```

So, here we got the depth information and we will read that as a list of Doubles. We will run the same command again, but now we will get the magnitude information, so we will have to pass 4 instead of 3:

```
In [20]:  readColumn (transpose southwest !! 4) :: [Double]
          [4.7,4.9,4.7,4.3,4.8,4.6,5.8,6.0,5.0,4.7,4.4,4.6,5.3,5.1,5.1,4.2,4.6,4.4,4.3,4.5,4.8,5.2,4.9,5.9,5.2,4.3,5.0,4.7]
```

This is all of our magnitude information for earthquakes in the southern hemisphere. Now, you'll notice that there doesn't seem to be any order to our information here, so let's do another southwest query. We're going to use what's known as the ORDER BY:

```
In [21]:  southwest <- quickQuery db "SELECT * FROM earthquakes WHERE latitude < 0 AND longitude < 0 ORDER BY magnitude" []
```

So, now our southwest is going to be ordered by magnitude.

```
In [22]:  readColumn (transpose southwest !! 4) :: [Double]
          [4.2,4.3,4.3,4.3,4.4,4.4,4.5,4.6,4.6,4.6,4.7,4.7,4.7,4.7,4.8,4.8,4.9,4.9,5.0,5.0,5.1,5.1,5.2,5.2,5.3,5.8,5.9,6.0]
```

If you read the fourth column again, you can quickly see that the smallest-magnitude earthquake in the southwest hemisphere was 4.2 and the largest is 6.0. By combining with the LIMIT command, it would simply mean order by magnitude, but take the first five. Here is the statement:

```
In [23]:  southwest <- quickQuery db "SELECT * FROM earthquakes WHERE latitude < 0 AND longitude < 0 ORDER BY magnitude LIMIT 5" []
```

So now, whenever we read our columns again of the southwest hemisphere we should only get five values, and they're going to be the five smallest-value earthquakes, as shown as follows:

```
In [24]:  readColumn (transpose southwest !! 4) :: [Double]
          [4.2,4.3,4.3,4.3,4.4]
```

But, what if we want to flip this on its head and get the five largest earthquakes? Well, that's a simple change. We're going to expand on our query statement once again and after the magnitude, but before the LIMIT we will add DESC, and that stands for descending:

```
In [25]:  southwest <- quickQuery db "SELECT * FROM earthquakes WHERE latitude < 0 AND longitude < 0 ORDER BY magnitude DESC LIMIT 5
```

This will sort the magnitudes from largest to smallest, and then take the first five. So, we're going to run the transpose statement again and check what we get:

```
In [26]:  readColumn (transpose southwest !! 4) :: [Double]
          [6.0,5.9,5.8,5.3,5.2]
```

It works, we see the top 5 magnitudes.

So, in this section, all that we did was we took the SELECT query and we started molding it using the WHERE clause. After we experimented with a few circumstances in which we sliced up the data with WHERE, we began to sort that data based on one of the columns; and in this particular instance, it was by magnitude. Afterward, we looked at how we could order by the magnitude either from smallest to largest—which is the default—or from largest to smallest; and that requires us to add the DESC call.

We can get a finer-grained selection to our data, and with the `LIMIT` call, we can prevent ourselves from getting so much data that we can't work with it. If you feel like you're getting too much data, you can add that `LIMIT` to your `SELECT` query, but Haskell can handle as much as you can throw at it, depending on the memory of your system. In the next section, we will be looking at how to incorporate our descriptive statistics module with the material that we've covered in this section.

Working with SQLite3 and descriptive statistics

So far, we've seen how to generate an SQLite3 database using the sqlite3 command-line utility, and how to interact with that database within Haskell. This section combines the knowledge of descriptive statistics from Chapter 1, *Descriptive Statistics*, with our database work in Chapter 2, *SQLite3*. We will be using descriptive statistics with our SQLite3 database in this section. First, we will create our descriptive statistics module from functions found in our Baseball notebook. Second, we will slice up some data using `SELECT` queries. Third, we will pass data to our descriptive statistics functions, and discuss the results. We'll be looking at earthquakes, specifically in the region of Oklahoma. So, let's glide over to our virtual machine running our IHaskell Notebook, and what I would like to do is to discuss how we can take the functions that we wrote in Chapter 1, *Descriptive Statistics*, related to our baseball data, and how we can use it here. So, let's go to our analysis folder in which we keep all of our notebooks; I have added a file called `DescriptiveStats.hs`:

```
jcchurch@dataanalysis:~/Code/HaskellDataAnalysis/analysis$ ls
Baseball.ipynb          Baseball-OpenCSV.ipynb        Earthquakes.ipynb
Baseball-Mean.ipynb     Baseball-Range.ipynb          Earthquakes-SELECT.ipynb
Baseball-Median.ipynb   DescriptiveStats.hs
Baseball-Mode.ipynb     Earthquakes-Connect.ipynb
jcchurch@dataanalysis:~/Code/HaskellDataAnalysis/analysis$
```

I have highlighted the file; you should create a file called `DescriptiveStats.hs`, and you should take all of the functions that we wrote in our Baseball notebook and add them to this file. So, if you open and look at this file, you will that we have got our `range`, `mean`, `stdev`, `median`, `countLeader`, `countPairs`, and `mode` functions. So, these were the functions that we wrote. Now, in order to make this a full-fledged module, we're going to add our module line at the start of the file, as shown in the following screenshot:

```
module DescriptiveStats where

import Data.List
import Data.Ord
import Data.Maybe

range :: Ord a => [a] -> Maybe (a, a)
range [] = Nothing
range [x] = Just (x, x)
range xs = Just (minimum xs, maximum xs)

mean :: Real a => [a] -> Maybe Double
mean []  = Nothing
mean [x] = Just $ realToFrac x
mean xs  = Just $ realToFrac (sum xs) / fromIntegral (length xs)

stdev :: Real a => [a] -> Maybe Double
stdev []  = Nothing
stdev [_] = Nothing
stdev xs = Just $ sqrt (sumsquares / n_m1)
  where
    n_m1 = fromIntegral (length xs - 1)
```

As you can see, after the module line we have also written the import statements. Now, once you've completed that, you should have your `DescriptiveStats` module ready to go. So, let's go over to our notebook, and we are going to scroll up to the very top, and put the cursor in the very first cell up at the very top:

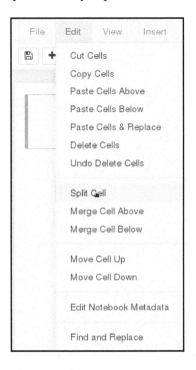

Now, we will go and click on **Edit | Split Cell**, and that's going to create a new cell before the import statements, as shown as follows:

In the new added first cell, we loaded our `DescriptiveStats` module. In our next block, added another import line where we import `DescriptiveStats`. Now that we've loaded the `DescriptiveStats` module and imported it, we are going to click on **Kernel | Restart & Run All**. This is going to reset the notebook and load our `DescriptiveStats` module, and re-import all of our imports. It's going to take a moment to wake up, and we're going to see it run. If you got any error messages from this step, chances are you mistyped something in the `DescriptiveStats.hs` file. You can always pull the `DescriptiveStats.hs` file that we have shared with this book. All right, we're all set to try to answer a question. So, what we would like to do is look at the state of Oklahoma:

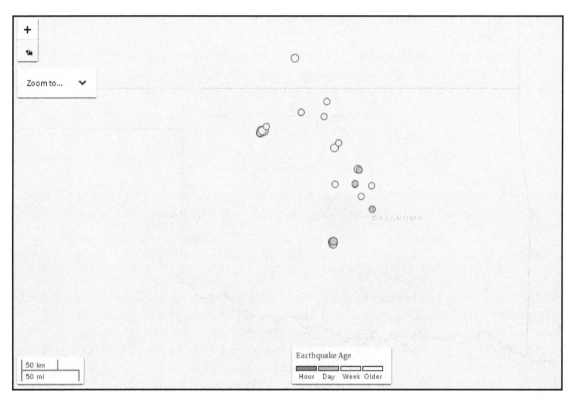

There are many earthquakes around the world. We could simply compute the average over all of them in the past week, but we would like to focus in on Oklahoma. Oklahoma is situated between 33.5 degrees north and 37 degrees north, as well as 94.3 degrees west and 100 degrees west. For those of you who know about the shape of Oklahoma, I'm ignoring the rectangular portion on the left, known as the Panhandle, and I'm focusing just on the mainland, which encompasses most of the earthquakes that you see in the previous screenshot.

Now, earthquakes in Oklahoma are an interesting phenomenon. Historically, major earthquakes don't happen in Oklahoma, but Oklahoma is a special case. Recent years have brought the practice called fracking to Oklahoma. Fracking damages the earth, and it's believed that this is the cause of the increase in earthquakes. While we don't have access to years of data in our 7-day database, let's look at the magnitude of Oklahoma earthquakes compared to non-Oklahoma earthquakes:

```
In [25]: oklahoma <- quickQuery db "SELECT * FROM earthquakes WHERE
latitude  > 33.5 AND latitude < 37 And longitude < -94.3  AND
longitude > -100 AND magnitude IS NOT ''" []
```

So, `oklahoma` is going to be a connection to our database. We are going to select all from earthquakes where the `latitude` is from `33.5` to `37` and the `longitude` is from `-94.3` to `-100`. Now, what I've noticed in the US Geological Survey database is that sometimes the magnitudes will appear blank, and so we have a called `magnitude IS NOT` blank. Let's hit *Shift + Enter* on this query, and we're going to see how many earthquakes we get:

```
In [26]: length oklahoma
              33
```

So, we got `33` earthquakes. What we will do next is to get everything that's not in the state of Oklahoma. So, we will copy our Oklahoma query, and will make a few changes:

```
In[27]: notoklahoma <- quickQuery db "SELECT * FROM earthquakes WHERE
Not(latitude  > 33.5 AND latitude < 37 And longitude < -94.3          AND
longitude > -100) AND magnitude IS NOT ''" []
```

So, we have changed `oklahoma` to `notoklahoma`, and we have introduced a new function, `NOT`, and wrapped all of the latitude and longitude coordinates in parentheses. We still include the `AND magnitude IS NOT` blank, but that's outside the latitude and longitude coordinates. So, what this says is if an earthquake exists inside the state of Oklahoma, we're going to exclude it, but if it's outside Oklahoma, we're going to include it. So, let's run that query, and see how many non-Oklahoma earthquakes we get:

```
In [28]: length notoklahoma
              1549
```

We got 1549 non-Oklahoma earthquakes. Now, in our dataset, we know that the fourth column - remembering that the first column is really the 0th column - is our magnitude, and we already know how to do that by using transpose, and we will save it in the okmag list and read it as a Double:

```
In [29]: okmag = readColumn (transpose oklahoma !! 4) :: [Double]
```

We also know that our non-Oklahoma earthquakes notokmag comes from notoklahoma, and it's also on the 4:

```
In [30]: notokmag = readColumn (transpose notoklahoma !! 4) :: [Double]
```

Now, here's where I believe that we could have some fun. We simply pass these lists okmag and notokmag to our functions found in the descriptive statistics module.

So, the mean of okmag and notokamg would be as follows:

```
In [31]: mean okmag
         Just 2.8424242424242423
In [32]: mean notokmag
         Just 1.4760490639122006
```

The average magnitude earthquake for okmag was 2.84, and for notokmag it was 1.47. So, earthquakes inside of Oklahoma have a higher magnitude than earthquakes outside of Oklahoma. Now, does this stack up with the information provided by the median? The median gets the true middle based on the amount of data that we have. So, let's check out the median for both okmag and notokmag:

```
In [33]: median okmag
         Just 2.7
In [34]: median notokmag
         Just 1.2
```

We got `2.74` inside of Oklahoma, and `1.24` outside of Oklahoma. Now, which of these two states has the larger variation of earthquake magnitudes? Let's find out:

```
In [35]: stdev okmag

         Just 0.5798870057122676

In [36]: stdev notokmag

         Just 1.1934121006742073
```

We see a standard deviation of `0.58` inside Oklahoma, and `1.19` outside Oklahoma. So, there's a higher standard deviation among non-Oklahoma earthquakes as opposed to Oklahoma earthquakes.

Since we are testing out different functions, let's go ahead and test out the `mode` function too. So, what is the most frequently seen magnitude across all of our data for the two datasets?

```
In [37]: mode okmag

         Just (2.5,7)

In [38]: mode notokmag

         Just (1.2,47)
```

So, for Oklahoma, 7 earthquakes have a magnitude of 2.5, and for states outside Oklahoma, 47 earthquakes have a magnitude of just 1.2. We could further slice up our data based on the depth of these earthquakes, and we can study that information, but I believe that this is a good example of how to use descriptive statistics with the SQLite3 database.

Summary

In this chapter, we installed the sqlite3 command-line utility and installed the necessary SQLite3 libraries for working with data in the IHaskell environment. Most data doesn't come in SQLite3 format, but in CSV format. So, we covered how to convert a CSV file into an SQLite3 table. We explored the versatility of SELECT queries in SQLite3 by means of the WHERE clause, the ORDER BY clause, and the LIMIT clause. We also explored how to create our own custom module of descriptive statistics, and then we used that module in order to study earthquake data in the IHaskell environment. In our next chapter, we're going to take a look at regular expressions in Haskell.

3
Regular Expressions

In this chapter, we are going to learn and understand what regular expressions are. The purpose of regular expressions is to represent a pattern that can be identified within some text data. In the context of data analysis, there are a couple of important uses for regular expressions:

- To validate fields to make sure that all values within a particular column adhere to a particular format
- To search fields based on a particular pattern

Word processors and editing applications have a Find and Replace feature. You submit a bit of text to identify within a larger bit of text, and the desired replacement. The application will replace all of the found text with the desired text. Many of these applications now include regular expression support. Rather than submitting an exact sequence of characters that need to be found, we submit a pattern. This pattern defines what is considered valid or not, using regular expressions. So, regular expressions are a mini-language. They aren't limited to the Haskell language. Once you understand regular expressions, you should be able to translate that knowledge into other programming languages. Each programming language may implement the mini-language of regular expressions, with slight variations, so you'll need to properly test your expressions when moving from language to language.

In this chapter, we're going to understand the mini-language of regular expressions, which includes the following:

- Dots and pipes
- Atoms and atom modifiers
- Character classes
- Using regular expressions with a CSV file
- Using regular expressions with an SQLite3 database

Dots and pipes

In this section, we're going to cover two basic bits of regular expression syntax, and those are dots and pipes. So, to begin, we are going to install the regular expression library in Haskell, and we are going to introduce the dot and the pipe syntax. Let's find the Terminal, and we need to begin by installing the library, which can be done with the following command:

```
jcchurch@dataanalysis:~/Code/HaskellDataAnalysis/analysis$ cabal install regex-p
osix
```

So, `cabal install regex-posix` will install our regular expression library. Now, once installed, let's go and create a new notebook, and dive in. We are going to name this notebook as `RegexLearning`. We need to import the `Text.Regex.Posix` library, so that we can access the `=~` operator, which is necessary to look at regular expressions. Let's define a couple of strings in order to get us started:

```
In [1]:  import Text.Regex.Posix

In [2]:  str1 = "one fish two fish red fish blue fish"

In [3]:  str2 = "The quick brown fox jumps over the lazy dog."
```

As you can see, `str1` is `"one fish two fish red fish blue fish"`, the title of a popular Dr. Seuss book that I like to use when teaching regular expressions. The second string, `str2`, is going to be a classic: `"The quick brown fox jumps over the lazy dog."`. Now that we have a couple of strings and we have our library imported, we now have access to the `=~` operator, which can be used to evaluate whether a pattern exists in a string. So, let's do a few quick examples. The first example is going to be very simple; we need to check whether a string exists inside of another string:

```
In [4]:  str1 =~ "one" :: Bool
         True
```

What we are asking here is, does the substring one exist inside of str1? And, we can see that it is **True**. Now, let's do this again with str2:

```
In [5]:  str2 =~ "one" :: Bool
         False
```

We are checking whether the same string, one, exists in str2. The result is **False** as there is no such string in str2.

Now, let's go over our first bit of regular expression syntax, which is the **dot**, also called the period. The dot matches any one character. So, we know that the word one exists in str1, but what about a different expression? So, let's say the following:

```
In [6]:  str1 =~ "o.e" :: Bool
         True

In [7]:  str2 =~ "o.e" :: Bool
         True
```

So, what we're asking here is, does the sequence o followed by the character e exist in str1? Well, we already know we have the word one in str1 where this condition is true, hence the output is **True**. We did the same thing for the str2 string, and that too came out to be **True** because the letters o and e in the word over exist inside str2.

The second regular expression character that we would like to introduce in this section is the **pipe**. The pipe character is made using the vertical character or bar that appears over the *Enter* key on most keyboards. Many programming languages use the pipe to represent OR, and regular expressions are no different. We can put a pipe between two expressions, and that means that either the first or the second expression is valid. So, let's do a quick example:

```
In [8]:  str1 =~ "fish|fox" :: Bool
         True

In [9]:  str2 =~ "fish|fox" :: Bool
         True
```

In this first case, we are checking whether the word `fish` or `fox` appears in our string `str1`. We know that the word `fish` appears several times in our first string, so it will return **True**. We also did the same with `str2` and we know that the word `fox` appears in our second string. So, of course, this also results in a **True**.

We can try out one more example and check for whether the word `dog` or `cat` exists in our strings, `str1` and `str2`:

```
In [10]:  str1 =~ "dog|cat" :: Bool
          False

In [11]:  str1 =~ "dog|cat" :: Bool
          False
```

As you can see, both of these are going to result in **False**.

So, in this section, we installed the regular expression library and we looked at two symbols within the regular expression syntax: the dot and the pipe. The dot represents any one character, and the pipe means that any two expressions can be true. We could also chain multiple expressions with pipe so that any one of the expressions in the pipe chain can be true. In our next section, we will be looking at simple modifiers with regular expressions, and understand what an atom is.

Atom and Atom modifiers

In this section, we will be expanding on our knowledge of regular expressions by discussing the atom. We will be covering the concept of an atom. An atom is a single expression such as a character or a dot, or an expression that has been defined using parentheses or - as we will see in a further section- the character class. We will also introduce atom modifiers. The idea is that you can take any atom, and then modify it using a modifier. Now, let's go back to our RegexLearning notebook and continue from where we left off in the last section.

Imagine that you have a string representing a date in the year-month-day separated by a dashes format, and you wish to verify that this date is in the 1900s or the 2000s. So, let's say that we have a date of 1969-07-20, and we wish to verify that this date is in either the 1900s or the 2000s:

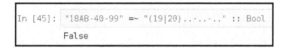

Well, we crafted a regular expression based on an atom of 19|20 followed by a series of dots, and then dashes separating those dots for the remainder part of the string, then checked the Bool value. In this case, we got a **True** as 1969 belongs to the 1900s.

Let's test it for a different date, say, 18AB-40-99. This is another date that could potentially enter into a system by a stretch of the imagination, and let's see if this is valid in the same regular expression:

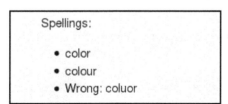

This came out to be **False**. As you can see, this regular expression only validates the first two digits with the 19|20 atom. This isn't a perfect regular expression because it doesn't validate the entire date, but we'll build on this particular expression as we progress. For now, let's hold on to this example; it will get better. This idea however lends itself to the concept of atom modifications. So, with atom modifiers, we can specify how many times an atom should be repeated inside of an expression.

Let's change the next block in our notebook to a markdown. We can modify any atom using symbols after the atom. For example, how do you spell the word "color"? Let's see the following screenshot:

Spellings:

- color
- colour
- Wrong: coluor

As you can see in American English, we spell it as `color`, whereas there are other parts of the world that spell it `colour`. However, we know for a fact that `coluor` is the wrong spelling.

Using the `?` regular expression, we can specify that the u is optional, and that either spelling with the u or without the u is legal as long as that u appears after the o. So, let's define our regular expression:

```
In [46]:  "color" =~ "colou?r" :: Bool
          True
```

We have the American spelling, `color`, on the left and the one with u on the right. As you can see, there is a question mark that appears after the atom u, meaning that the u is now optional. Hence, the result comes out to be **True**. Let's take the same expression and modify it a bit:

```
In [47]:  "colour" =~ "colou?r" :: Bool
          True
```

So, we have replaced `color` with `colour` on the left. This expression still comes out to **True**. Now, let's mispell the word and check the `Bool` value:

```
In [48]:  "coluor" =~ "colou?r" :: Bool
          False
```

So, instead of ou, we have uo now, and it results in **False** because the u didn't appear in the correct place.

Now, let's look at our next two modifiers. For example, imagine that you have a pattern that requires that we match a string containing any number of 1s followed by any number of 2s. The `*` character means that an atom must appear at a minimum of 0 times, or many times. So, let's see an example:

```
In [49]:  "1122" =~ "1*2*" :: Bool
          True
```

So, will `1122` match a pattern of any number of 1s followed by any number of 2s? The result is **True**. Well, let's say we just have an empty string. Will that also meet the pattern of any number of 1s followed by any number of 2s?

```
In [50]:  "" =~ "1*2*" :: Bool
          True
```

Yes it does, because any number could also mean `0`.

What if we just leave 1 out, for example, `111`? See the following:

```
In [51]:  "111" =~ "1*2*" :: Bool
          True
```

That too results in **True**.

What about something that has nothing to do with 1s or 2s at all?

```
In [52]:  "ABC" =~ "1*2*" :: Bool
          True
```

Yes, all of these are **True**. In fact, you'll notice all of these expressions that we've gone through are **True**. It's not possible for us to write a string that fails on this particular regular expression. Now, let's change this up, and say that the 1s and 2s in this string have to appear at least once, but they can still appear any number of times. Well, we just change those * characters to + signs. Let's see a few examples:

```
In [53]:  "1122" =~ "1+2+" :: Bool
          True

In [54]:  "11" =~ "1+2+" :: Bool
          False

In [55]:  "12" =~ "1+2+" :: Bool
          True
```

The first case came out **True** because we have at least one of each character. But, if we leave out one character or the other, as you can see in the second previous input box , you'll see that it returns **False**. At a minimum, we must have one of each in order for the expression to be **True**, as seen in the third input box.

Finally, we have something known as the custom modifier, which will allow you to create custom specifications based on any number of repetitions. So, for now a convoluted example. Let's say that we want the number 1 followed by the number 2, which must appear between 3 and 5 times, followed by the number 3. If your string is 123, the following results:

```
In [56]:  "123" =~ "12{3,5}3" :: Bool
            False
```

In order to create a custom modification, we pass in high and low values in curly braces. So, this says that the 2 must appear between 3 and 5 times; and we see that the 2 only appears once in our original string, so this fails. Hence, we get **False**.

If we repeat this again with just two 2s, we see that also will also result in **False**, as seen in the following screenshot:

```
In [57]:  "1223" =~ "12{3,5}3" :: Bool
            False
```

But, once we enter three 2s into our expression, we will see that it will give us **True**:

```
In [58]:  "12223" =~ "12{3,5}3" :: Bool
            True
```

Since this is a custom modification, where we say at most 5, and if I enter six 2s, this is going to fail:

```
In [59]:  "12222223" =~ "12{3,5}3" :: Bool
            False
```

So, those were the four modifiers that we covered in this section. We've covered the ?, which can appear 0 or 1 times. We've covered the *, which can appear 0 to many times. We've covered the + sign, which can cover one to many times; and then we have the custom modifier, which is based on our own criteria.

Any expression that's been modified with a minimum number of 0 required matches, such as the ?, the *, or a specified modifier with 0 minimum matches, will always evaluate to **True**. You need to be mindful of your expression so that if all of your atoms are modified in this manner, your expression will always be **True**, and then your expression is not useful to you.

In the next section, we're going to introduce character classes.

Character classes

Character classes are a way of combining characters with common traits into a single classification, such as characters that represent numbers, letters, vowels, or hexadecimal characters. Once we get into the details, we will see how useful character classes are. So, in this section, we're going to take a look at introducing the basics of character classes. We'll expound on that by introducing character class ranges, character class negations, and then we will write a full regular expression to handle matching dates.

So, our first introduction to character classes begins with vowels. Vowels are the letters A, E, I, O, U. Almost every word has a vowel in it. Let's see if we can write a character class that matches a vowel:

```
In [36]:  "dog" =~ "[aeiou]" :: Bool
              True
```

So, here we have word "dog" and, to begin a character class, we use square braces. Inside the square braces we have our vowels, aeiou, and we're going to match that to a Bool. Now, a character class means that a letter must match one of the letters that exist in those square brackets.

For this case, there is a vowel in the word `dog`, so this results in **True**. Let's try another word, for example, `why`:

```
In [37]:  "why" =~ "[aeiou]" :: Bool
          False
```

This turns out to be **False**. There are no vowels in the word `why`. As long as one character inside the character class matches, the entire character class matches.

Now, we will create a character class for numbers. So, in the string `"123"`, we could ask whether that string contains any numbers? This will require us to create a character class consisting of the digits 0 to 9:

```
In [38]:  "123" =~ "[0123456789]" :: Bool
          True
```

That resulted in **True**. Let's do the same thing with `dog`:

```
In [39]:  "dog" =~ "[0123456789]" :: Bool
          False
```

We see that it gives **False**. We could also create a character class for letters of the alphabet where we would type `abcd`, all the way to the letter `z`, but that would be very error-prone. If you missed a letter, that letter would never be matched in the character class. For this reason, character classes support ranges. Inside of the character class, use a hyphen between two characters and you will get all of the characters, from the first character to the second. As you can see in our examples, character classes are not case-sensitive. So, let's go through a few examples. We will take one of our previous examples:

```
In [40]:  "123" =~ "[0-9]" :: Bool
          True
```

We can see that adding a range of 0-9 worked, and we got **True**. We could also do the same for the word `dog` and check whether it contains any lowercase letters:

```
In [41]:  "dog" =~ "[a-z]" :: Bool
          True
```

Of course, it does. So, this results in **True**. Let's do the same thing again, but we are checking for uppercase letters now in the word `dog`:

```
In [42]:  "dog" =~ "[A-Z]" :: Bool
          False
```

We see that it does not match, hence we got **False**.

In order to find words with mixed cases in a character class, you simply repeat two ranges back-to-back, once for uppercase and again for lowercase. Let's check for the word `DoG`:

```
In [43]:  "DoG" =~ "[A-Za-z]" :: Bool
          True
```

It returned **True**. Now, one more feature of character classes needs to be expressed, and that is the negative character class, which matches to any character not found in the character class. To make a negative character class, start the first character in the character class with ^. So, let's check if the word `why` contains any constant sounds:

```
In [44]:  "why" =~ "[^aeiou]" :: Bool
          True
```

As you can see, in the character class, the very first character is ^ followed by the vowels, `aeiou`. So, this means no vowels; in other words, anything that's not a vowel. And, it is **True** as there are characters that are not vowels in the word `why`.

What about any symbols that aren't letters of the alphabet? There is a singer in America by the name of Kesha, and Kesha spells her name `Ke$ha`. What we would like to ask is, does Kesha's name have any non-letter characters? We will be using the ^ character:

```
In [45]:  "Ke$ha" =~ "[^A-Za-z]" :: Bool
          True
```

We can see that she does have a non-letter character, hence it returned **True**.

Remember in our last section, where we talked about how to express a date and we talked about expressing a date that only works for the 1900s or the 2000s. So, let's say that we have a date, 1969-07-20, and we would like to express that if that truly is a date. To verify that, let's have a regular expression to match a date, and we will use lots of character classes to make sure that we put numbers into our expressions correctly:

```
In [46]:  date1 = "1969-07-20"

In [47]:  date1 =~ "(19|20)[0-9][0-9]-[0-9][0-9]-[0-9][0-9]" :: Bool
          True
```

So, we begin with 19|20, followed by two numbers and then a dash; and then two numbers and then a dash; and then two numbers. We can see that the result is **True**. So, let's play around with this expression. We will copy the same expression, and we're going to check for a different date, say, 1901-40-99:

```
In [48]:  "1901-40-99" =~ "(19|20)[0-9][0-9]-[0-9][0-9]-[0-9][0-9]" :: Bool
          True
```

We see that it is also **True**, so this doesn't work perfectly for all dates. Let's see if we can modify this scanning so that we resolve this to be **False**. Now, a month can only be the numbers 01 all the way up to 12, for January to December. So, we are going to modify the month portion in our regular expression:

```
In [49]:  "1901-40-99" =~ "(19|20)[0-9][0-9]-(0[1-9]|1[012])-[0-9][0-9]" :: Bool
          False
```

So, we will take 0 followed by a character class of 1–9, or a 1 followed by the character class of 012. So, here we have a character class that matches just the digits 01 all the way up to 12. We got a **False** for 40, which doesn't qualify as a valid month. Now, this still doesn't work because we have 99 on the end, although that still results in a **False**. Now, in order to get that last date, we need to make sure that we only allow for days of the month that go from 01 all the way up to 31. So, let's elaborate on that:

```
In [50]:  "1901-40-99" =~ "(19|20)[0-9][0-9]-(0[1-9]|1[012])-(0[1-9]|[12][0-9]|3[01])" :: Bool

          False
```

We have our 0 followed by 1–9, or we can have a 1 or a 2 that goes from 0–9, followed by another |, and a 3, which can have a 0 or a 1 after it. This is a very lengthy regular expression to match a day of the week. We see that it also resulted in **False**.

Now, we should test this under a variety of circumstances, but we are going to test this out again with our original date of 1969-07-20:

```
In [51]:  date1 =~ "(19|20)[0-9][0-9]-(0[1-9]|1[012])-(0[1-9]|[12][0-9]|3[01])" :: Bool

          True
```

This one is still **True**. So, at least we know that this regular expression works for these two circumstances, and we would need further testing in order to verify this one. Regular expressions can be very hairy and they can also be very hard to test, but once you figure out the language, you can do lots with them. So, in our next section, we are going to use regular expressions in the context of a CSV file.

Regular expressions in CSV files

We need to know the importance of using regular expressions in various file formats such as CSV and SQLite3. In this section, we will be covering the CSV format. So, let's examine a question using one of our past datasets. Using our Baseball dataset, let's try to find out the average number of runs scored by away teams in the month of March. To do this, we'll need our CSV file of data, which has the dates in the first column, but is not organized by month.

So, in order to solve this, we're going to be crafting a regular expression to match a field in the CSV file. In this case, we will be using the first column of dates. We're going to be pairing that information with another column; and in this case, the other column is going to be the runs scored by away teams. Then, we're going to filter that information to get just the information that corresponds to the regular expression.

For this section, I have created a file called `MyCSV.hs`. You can find it in the source code folder, which is provided with this book. Let's check the file:

```
module MyCSV where

import Text.CSV

noEmptyRows :: Either a CSV -> CSV
noEmptyRows ecsv = either (const []) (filter (\row -> 2 <= length row)) ecsv

{- Reads a column of data from a CSV file -}
readIndex :: Read cell => Either a CSV -> Int -> [cell]
readIndex ecsv index = map read (getIndex ecsv index)

{- Reads a column of data from a CSV file -}
getIndex :: Either a CSV -> Int -> [String]
getIndex ecsv index = map (!! index) (noEmptyRows ecsv)




"MyCSV.hs" 14 lines, 451 characters
```

As you can see, I've created a module of the functions that we utilized in Chapter 1, *Descriptive Statistics*, such as the `noEmptyRows` function and the `readIndex` function. I've also included a function called `getIndex`. Now, `readIndex` is a partial function that allows us to parse data from a column; whereas `getIndex` simply returns information from a column as is, in the string format. So, let's create a new notebook called `RegexLearning-CSV` utilizing `MyCSV`. First, we need to load up our `DescriptiveStats` and `MyCSV` libraries:

```
In [1]:  :load DescriptiveStats
         :load MyCSV
```

Now, let's do our imports:

```
In [2]:  import Text.CSV
         import Data.Maybe
         import Text.Regex.Posix
         import DescriptiveStats
         import MyCSV
```

We will be utilizing the `Text.CSV`, `Data.Maybe`, regular expressions, and then finally, the two libraries that are custom-made for this section. Now, we need to parse our CSV file, and we're going to use the exact same dataset that we used in `Chapter 1`, Descriptive Statistics, the Baseball dataset:

```
In [3]:  baseball <- parseCSVFromFile "../data/GL2015.TXT"
```

Now, we need to get the game dates. And, if you recall, all of the game dates were in the first column, and so that means column 0:

```
In [4]:  gameDates = getIndex baseball 0
```

Now, let's look at the first entry in `gameDates`:

```
In [5]:  head gameDates
             "20150405"
```

We see the date here is March 5th 2015, but it's one long string of numbers. What we need to do now is to craft a regular expression to get just the 04 portion of that. So, let's create `marchDates`, and this is going to be a Boolean array of length equal to `gameDates`; it will be **True** if it's in the month of March, and it will be **False** otherwise:

```
In [6]:  marchDates = map (=~ "....04..") gameDates :: [Bool]
```

So, we have mapped our regular expression function, and we have passed in a regular expression of 04. We have added 4 dots at the beginning because we don't care about the year, we have 04 because we care about the month of March, and then 2 more dots afterward because we're not worried about the day. We have then passed in **gameDates**.

We also need the awayRuns that we've used in an earlier section:

```
In [7]:  awayRuns = readIndex baseball 9 :: [Integer]
```

If you recall, those are going to be on the 10th column, so we have passed in 9 for the index; and parsed as Integer. Next, we need to make sure that the length of marchDates and the length of awayRuns are identical:

```
In [8]:  length marchDates

         2429

In [9]:  length awayRuns

         2429
```

Well, they both match, we got 2429 games. Now, what we need to do is combine these two datasets; let's do that by running the following command:

```
In [10]:  zip marchDates awayRuns
          [(True,3),(True,0),(True,0),(True,1),(True,6),(True,0),(True,1),(True,6),(True,5),(True,2),(True,3),(True,2),(True,10),(T
          rue,8),(True,3),(True,3),(True,2),(True,6),(True,6),(True,7),(True,12),(True,5),(True,0),(True,2),(True,5),(True,3),(True
          ,0),(True,5),(True,0),(True,5),(True,0),(True,4),(True,4),(True,2),(True,5),(True,2),(True,1),(True,1),(True,5),(True,1),
          (True,6),(True,10),(True,2),(True,6),(True,1),(True,6),(True,4),(True,12),(True,6),(True,8),(True,6),(True,0),(True,5),(T
          rue,3),(True,3),(True,4),(True,1),(True,9),(True,6),(True,1),(True,0),(True,6),(True,1),(True,4),(True,9),(True,8),(True,
          5),(True,2),(True,0),(True,3),(True,4),(True,9),(True,2),(True,0),(True,2),(True,2),(True,9),(True,10),(True,2),(True,8),
          (True,4),(True,8),(True,6),(True,7),(True,4),(True,7),(True,6),(True,8),(True,10),(True,4),(True,4),(True,6),(True,4),(Tr
          ue,8),(True,12),(True,6),(True,2),(True,2),(True,6),(True,5),(True,0),(True,4),(True,8),(True,2),(True,5),(True,3),(True,
          7),(True,4),(True,4),(True,2),(True,3),(True,8),(True,3),(True,5),(True,5),(True,2),(True,1),(True,4),(True,5),(True,10),
          (True,2),(True,1),(True,1),(True,10),(True,7),(True,6),(True,0),(True,2),(True,1),(True,1),(True,2),(True,4),(True,2),(Tr
          ue,5),(True,4),(True,5),(True,7),(True,0),(True,2),(True,2),(True,1),(True,6),(True,4),(True,2),(True,3),(True,5),(True,8
          ),(True,5),(True,3),(True,1),(True,3),(True,9),(True,1),(True,2),(True,4),(True,12),(True,0),(True,5),(True,4),(True,1),(
          True,9),(True,5),(True,6),(True,3),(True,4),(True,2),(True,1),(True,2),(True,5),(True,8),(True,1),(True,3),(True,2),(True
          ,2),(True,10),(True,5),(True,5),(True,5),(True,0),(True,6),(True,2),(True,5),(True,1),(True,1),(True,6),(True,1),(True,3)
```

You're going to see the pairing of all of this information. You see a series of **True** because this is a chronological dataset beginning in the month of March. If you scroll down, at some point they transition into **False** because we go into the next month.

Now, we need to filter these based on what's **True** in the first portion of every tuple:

```
In [11]:  filter fst (zip marchDates awayRuns)

          [(True,3),(True,0),(True,0),(True,1),(True,6),(True,0),(True,1),(True,6),(True,5),(True,2),(True,3),(True,2),(True,10),(T
          rue,8),(True,3),(True,3),(True,2),(True,6),(True,6),(True,7),(True,12),(True,5),(True,0),(True,2),(True,5),(True,3),(True
          ,0),(True,5),(True,0),(True,5),(True,0),(True,4),(True,4),(True,2),(True,5),(True,2),(True,1),(True,1),(True,5),(True,1),
          (True,6),(True,10),(True,2),(True,6),(True,1),(True,6),(True,4),(True,12),(True,6),(True,8),(True,6),(True,0),(True,5),(T
          rue,3),(True,3),(True,4),(True,1),(True,9),(True,6),(True,1),(True,0),(True,6),(True,1),(True,4),(True,9),(True,8),(True,
          5),(True,2),(True,0),(True,3),(True,4),(True,9),(True,2),(True,0),(True,2),(True,2),(True,9),(True,10),(True,2),(True,8),
          (True,4),(True,8),(True,6),(True,7),(True,4),(True,7),(True,6),(True,8),(True,10),(True,4),(True,4),(True,6),(True,4),(Tr
          ue,8),(True,12),(True,6),(True,2),(True,2),(True,6),(True,5),(True,0),(True,4),(True,8),(True,2),(True,5),(True,3),(True,
          7),(True,4),(True,4),(True,2),(True,3),(True,8),(True,3),(True,5),(True,5),(True,2),(True,1),(True,4),(True,5),(True,10),
          (True,2),(True,1),(True,1),(True,10),(True,7),(True,6),(True,0),(True,2),(True,1),(True,1),(True,2),(True,4),(True,2),(Tr
          ue,5),(True,4),(True,5),(True,7),(True,0),(True,2),(True,2),(True,1),(True,6),(True,4),(True,2),(True,3),(True,5),(True,8
          ),(True,5),(True,3),(True,1),(True,3),(True,9),(True,1),(True,2),(True,4),(True,12),(True,0),(True,5),(True,4),(True,1),(
          True,9),(True,5),(True,6),(True,3),(True,4),(True,2),(True,1),(True,2),(True,5),(True,8),(True,1),(True,3),(True,2),(True
          ,2),(True,10),(True,5),(True,5),(True,5),(True,0),(True,6),(True,2),(True,5),(True,1),(True,1),(True,6),(True,1),(True,3)
          ,(True,1),(True,1),(True,7),(True,14),(True,6),(True,5),(True,1),(True,6),(True,5),(True,5),(True,6),(True,1),(True,6),(T
```

So here, `fst` stands for first, and then we pass in our combined datasets: `marchDates` and `awayRuns`. This produces just the list of elements that are in the month of March. You'll see it's a much shorter list, and the beginning of every tuple is **True**. Now, we need to strip out those Trues as they are 9no longer necessary. For that, we are going to use the following command:

```
In [12]:  map snd (filter fst (zip marchDates awayRuns))

          [3,0,0,1,6,0,1,6,5,2,3,2,10,8,3,3,2,6,6,7,12,5,0,2,5,3,0,5,0,5,0,4,4,2,5,2,1,1,5,1,6,10,2,6,1,6,4,12,6,8,6,0,5,3,3,4,1,9,
          6,1,0,6,1,4,9,8,5,2,0,3,4,9,2,0,2,2,9,10,2,8,4,8,6,7,4,7,6,8,10,4,4,6,4,8,12,6,2,2,6,5,0,4,8,2,5,3,7,4,4,2,3,8,3,5,5,2,1,
          4,5,10,2,1,1,10,7,6,0,2,1,1,2,4,2,5,4,5,7,0,2,2,1,6,4,2,3,5,8,5,3,1,3,9,1,2,4,12,0,5,4,1,9,5,6,3,4,2,1,2,5,8,1,3,2,2,10,5
          ,5,5,0,6,2,5,1,1,6,1,3,1,1,7,14,6,5,1,6,5,5,6,1,6,7,7,16,1,3,9,2,1,9,0,13,3,2,5,2,5,4,2,2,6,3,2,7,0,3,2,1,6,1,2,3,9,4,2,4
          ,2,7,2,13,1,5,0,3,4,7,4,2,3,0,3,1,4,1,8,9,8,2,2,5,0,5,5,11,5,7,3,6,4,7,4,1,8,5,2,3,4,1,5,6,5,1,3,5,4,0,6,3,3,9,4,11,11,2,
          2,2,2,5,13,2,2,2,3,14,5,2,1,5,10,3,6,5,1,13,8,8,3,3,7,2,5,2,1,2,6,5,8,3]
```

So, we have used `map snd` (snd for second), and passed in our expression. This will give us all the away runs scored in the month of March. Finally, we can take this expression and we can pass it to the mean:

```
In [13]:  mean $ map snd (filter fst (zip marchDates awayRuns))

          Just 4.2782874617737
```

So, we can say that an average of `4.2` runs was scored by away teams in the month of March. Hopefully, you can identify how this approach can be adapted to a solution that works for every month of the year. With a little more effort, we can examine the month with the highest and lowest average. In our next section, we are going to use regular expressions with SQLite3.

SQLite3 and regular expressions

Working with regular expressions in our SQLite3 database is no different than working with a CSV file. In this section, we will demonstrate how to filter our data using regular expressions, using the timestamp data from an SQLite3 database in a similar manner to our last section. So, we're going to be loading the data from the SQLite3 database, sifting through that data using a regular expression, and analyzing the data gleaned from that regular expression. Now, the problem that we will try to solve in this section is to determine how many earthquakes happen by hour in our 7-day database. Let's go and create a new Haskell notebook; we will name this notebook RegexLearning-SQLite3. Let's first import our libraries:

```
In [1]:   import Text.Printf
          import Text.Regex.Posix
          import Database.HDBC.Sqlite3
          import Database.HDBC
          import Data.List
```

We won't be using any descriptive statistics in this section, so there's no need to load the descriptive statistics module. There is one import that you see here that we haven't covered yet, and that's Text.Printf. There's one little problem that we are going to solve using the printf function, and you'll see that coming up. So, let's import our Earthquakes database that we created in Chapter 2, *SQLite3*:

```
In [2]:   db <- connectSqlite3 "../data/usgs.sqlite3"
```

Now, we need the readColumn function that will allow us to read data from a column:

```
In [3]:   readColumn = map fromSql
```

Now that we have our database ready, we need to pull the raw timestamps:

```
In [4]:   timeRaw <- quickQuery db "SELECT time FROM earthquakes" []
```

This command will pull all of the earthquake times. Now, we need to convert this raw time data into a string, which we will call `timestamps`:

```
In [6]:  timestamps = readColumn $ head (transpose timeRaw) :: [String]
```

So, we're reading the column and getting the head of the transpose of our data, and this will all be parsed into a list of strings. Now, let's examine the first timestamp:

```
In [7]:  head timestamps
         "2016-07-11T19:44:16.470Z"
```

As you can see, we have a much more complicated timestamp than what we were working with in the last section. There's lots more information here to work with. So, what we would like to do is to extract the hour from each timestamp, and the hour occurs right after the letter T, and the two-digit number 19. So, here's where the `printf` function comes in. I would like to take any number and convert it to a two-digit number as a string with T in the front, and printf does this for me:

```
In [8]:  printf "T%02d" 7
         T07
```

I have passed in number 7, and it'll convert it to a two-digit number – zero-padded, with T in front. Likewise, we can try the number 19, and it will produce **T19**, as shown in the following screenshot:

```
In [9]:  printf "T%02d" 19
         T19
```

So, now that we have our raw timestamps converted to strings, we would like to be able to discern which timestamps have an hour that we are looking for, and which timestamps do not; and we can do that with regular expressions:

```
In [10]:  countAtHour :: Int -> Int
          countAtHour hour = length $ filter (=~ (printf "T%02d" hour :: String)) timestamps
```

So, `countAtHour` will be a function that takes an integer and returns an integer count of all of the earthquakes that happened at that hour. Then, `countAtHour` will take an `hour`, and we'll get the length of all of the data that matches the regular expression mentioned previously. We're basically going to filter anything that matches a regular expression defined by the return of the print statement, `T%02d`; then, we'll pass in our `hour` and make sure that is a `String`; and then, we will pass in our `timestamps`. Now, let's demonstrate how this works:

```
In [11]:  countAtHour 0
          76

In [12]:  countAtHour 1
          55

In [13]:  countAtHour 2
          52
```

So, `76` earthquakes happened at hour `0`. Similarly, we got `55` and `52` earhtquakes for hour `1` and hour `2` respectively. They will all be different based on your earthquake dataset. So, for our particular dataset, we got `76`, `55`, and `52`. Now, what we would like to do is to get all of the earthquakes by hour, and that is simple by mapping `countAtHour` to the range of numbers, `0` to `23`:

```
In [14]:  map countAtHour [0..23]
          [76,55,52,65,68,65,77,78,59,75,58,70,70,68,61,72,57,62,64,64,57,64,64,84]
```

We now got the full breadth of the 24-hour period from `0` to `23`. Next, we can bring in the descriptive statistics functions; and define the range and the standard deviation by hour. But hopefully, you can see how with this approach of using the regular expressions and the `printf` function, we have a lot of versatility in how we can find data in strings.

Summary

In this chapter, we began by installing the regular expression library, and we talked a little bit about the regular expression syntax, such as how the dot matches any one character and the pipe allows us to match any expression to the left or the right of the pipe. We talked about atoms and atom modifiers. We also talked about character classes at length. We used regular expressions within a CSV file and an SQLite3 database. You should always thoroughly test your regular expressions, as they tend to be difficult to debug. With that, we will be discussing data visualization in the next chapter.

4
Visualizations

In the previous chapter, we learned about regular expressions, and, in this chapter, we are going to talk all about visualizations. We will be covering the following topics:

- Installing the `gnuplot` command-line tool and `EasyPlot` Haskell library
- Plotting our first visualization
- Customizing a visualization to make it publication ready
- Adding multiple plots to a single visualization
- Learning about the importance of the moving average
- Learning about the importance of feature rescaling

Line plots of a single variable

In this section, we'll focus on an introduction to `EasyPlot`. So, we're going to be installing the `gnuplot` command-line tool and the `EasyPlot` Haskell library. `EasyPlot` is just a Haskell wrapper for `gnuplot`. It allows us to interact with the gnuplotting utility from within Haskell and our IHaskell environment. We need data, and for that we're going to be pulling data from Yahoo Finance. I like Yahoo Finance because I can obtain the full history of any publicly traded company; and in this section, we're going to end with our first plot. Let's go to our Terminal, but first we need to install `gnuplot`. The command is as follows:

```
jcchurch@dataanalysis:~/Downloads$ sudo apt-get install gnuplot
```

Now, let's do a cabal update and then cabal install `EasyPlot`, as shown in the following example:

```
jcchurch@dataanalysis:~/Downloads$ cabal update
Downloading the latest package list from hackage.haskell.org
jcchurch@dataanalysis:~/Downloads$ cabal install easyplot
Resolving dependencies...
cabal: Entering directory '/tmp/cabal-tmp-6405/easyplot-1.0'
Configuring easyplot-1.0...
Building easyplot-1.0...
Preprocessing library easyplot-1.0...
[1 of 1] Compiling Graphics.EasyPlot ( src/Graphics/EasyPlot.hs, dist/build/Grap
hics/EasyPlot.o )
Creating package registration file: /tmp/pkgConf-easyplot-16405.0
Installing library in
/home/jcchurch/.cabal/lib/x86_64-linux-ghc-7.6.3/easyplot-1.0-CcbZmtpoOwaLPtHw9r
xdq8
Registering easyplot-1.0...
cabal: Leaving directory '/tmp/cabal-tmp-6405/easyplot-1.0'
Installed easyplot-1.0
```

If you didn't get any error messages, that means you're ready to go. Now we need data; and, as I said earlier, I would like to use financial data from publicly traded companies on the New York Stock Exchange. For that, we're going to go to Yahoo Finance, and the first company that we would like to look at is Apple Corporation. You have to know the symbol for all the corporations in order to use Yahoo Finance, and the symbol for Apple is **AAPL**. So, type `aapl` into the search box and the first option is Apple, as shown in the following screenshot:

Once you click on AAPL, a page will open and you will see lots of information about the Apple stock, but what we are interested in is the **Historical Data**, so let's scroll down until we find the link for **Historical Data** and click on it, as shown in the following screenshot:

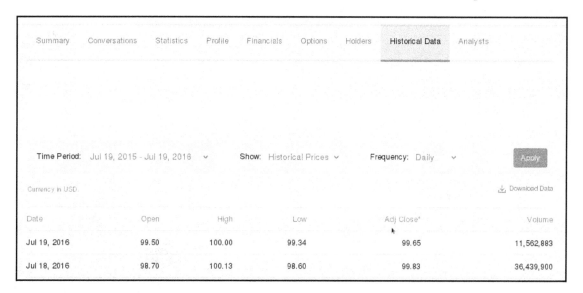

Once the page reloads, you're going to see one-year historical data for the stock. We are going to change the start and end dates for this range to be date well before the creation of the Apple company. So, we will say January 1, 1960. For the end date, we are going to select July 7, 2016. This is shown in the following screenshot:

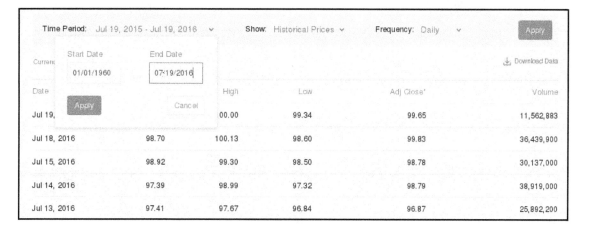

We need to hit **Apply**, and then we have to hit **Apply** again. Once the page reloads, you should see a link for **Download Data**. Let's click on it, and we can see that we have the ability to download a CSV file called `table.csv`. Let's go ahead and download that file, as shown in the following screenshot:

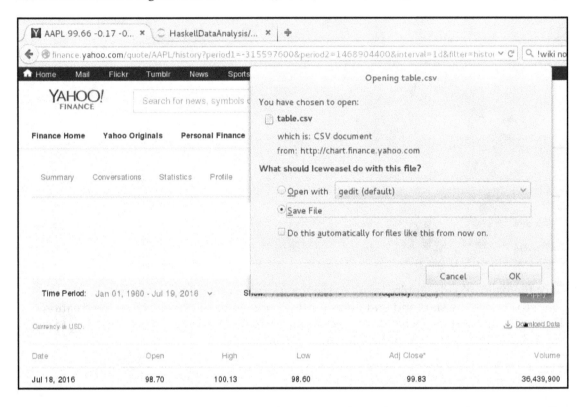

Let's change the filename that Yahoo provides to something that is more relevant. We will rename the file from `table.csv` to `aapl.csv`, by using the command shown in the following screenshot:

```
jcchurch@dataanalysis:~/Downloads$ ls
all_week.csv  earthquakes.csv  GL2015.TXT  gl2015.zip  table.csv  usgs.sqlite3
jcchurch@dataanalysis:~/Downloads$ mv table.csv aapl.csv
jcchurch@dataanalysis:~/Downloads$ vi aapl.csv ▮
```

Let's open the `aapl.csv` file, as shown in the following example:

```
Date,Open,High,Low,Close,Volume,Adj Close
2016-07-18,98.699997,100.129997,98.599998,99.830002,36439900,99.830002
2016-07-15,98.919998,99.300003,98.50,98.779999,29952500,98.779999
2016-07-14,97.389999,98.989998,97.32,98.790001,38348800,98.790001
2016-07-13,97.410004,97.669998,96.839996,96.870003,25655000,96.870003
2016-07-12,97.169998,97.699997,97.120003,97.419998,23889600,97.419998
2016-07-11,96.75,97.650002,96.730003,96.980003,23298900,96.980003
2016-07-08,96.489998,96.889999,96.050003,96.68,28855800,96.68
2016-07-07,95.699997,96.50,95.620003,95.940002,24280900,95.940002
2016-07-06,94.599998,95.660004,94.370003,95.529999,30770700,95.529999
2016-07-05,95.389999,95.400002,94.459999,95.040001,27257000,95.040001
2016-07-01,95.489998,96.470001,95.330002,95.889999,25872300,95.889999
2016-06-30,94.440002,95.769997,94.300003,95.599998,35119400,95.599998
2016-06-29,93.970001,94.550003,93.629997,94.400002,36427800,94.400002
2016-06-28,92.900002,93.660004,92.139999,93.589996,39311500,93.589996
2016-06-27,93.00,93.050003,91.50,92.040001,45489600,92.040001
2016-06-24,92.910004,94.660004,92.650002,93.400002,72894000,93.400002
2016-06-23,95.940002,96.290001,95.25,96.099998,31863500,96.099998
2016-06-22,96.25,96.889999,95.349998,95.550003,28971100,95.550003
2016-06-21,94.940002,96.349998,94.68,95.910004,35229500,95.910004
2016-06-20,96.00,96.57,95.029999,95.099998,33942300,95.099998
2016-06-17,96.620003,96.650002,95.300003,95.330002,60595000,95.330002
"aapl.csv" 8977 lines, 582517 characters
```

You can see that the CSV file has a header line, as well as several columns of information including the date, the volume, and the adjusted close. Now, the date column is a text field, the volume column is an integer field, and everything else is a floating-point field. You should also notice that this file is in reverse chronological order, which means the most recent date in the file is first, and the very last entry in the file is December 12, 1980, as can be seen in the following screenshot:

```
1980-12-23,30.874999,30.999999,30.874999,30.874999,11737600,0.463241
1980-12-22,29.625,29.75,29.625,29.625,9340800,0.444486
1980-12-19,28.249999,28.374999,28.249999,28.249999,12157600,0.423856
1980-12-18,26.625,26.75,26.625,26.625,18362400,0.399475
1980-12-17,25.875,25.999999,25.875,25.875,21610400,0.388222
1980-12-16,25.375,25.375,25.25,25.25,26432000,0.378845
1980-12-15,27.375001,27.375001,27.25,27.25,43971200,0.408852
1980-12-12,28.75,28.875,28.75,28.75,117258400,0.431358
```

The last record in this file is the first day of trading, and we see that the adjusted trade value on December 12, 1980 was 43 cents. The most recent adjusted close for Apple was 98 dollars and 83 cents. What I would like you to do now is to convert this file to a SQLite3 database. Also, I would like you to find two other companies on Yahoo Finance, and repeat this process so that you create a database containing three companies and their entire histories. I have already done this as a prework, and I have created a database containing Apple, Google, and Microsoft. You can choose any company from Yahoo Finance.

Let's go over to our Jupyter notebook. I have created a database called `stocks.sqlite3`, which is provided along with the files for this book, and it's already in my `data` folder, as demonstrated by the following screenshot:

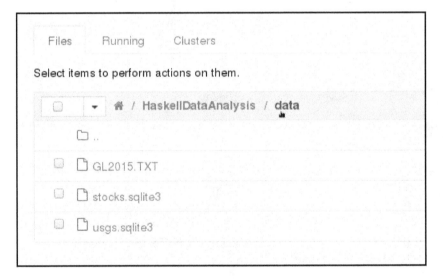

Let's begin with an analysis of that dataset. So, we will need to go back into our `analysis` folder. We're going to create a new Haskell notebook, and we'll call this `StockAnalysis`. Let's import a few libraries, as shown in following screenshot:

```
In [1]:  import Graphics.EasyPlot
         import Database.HDBC
         import Database.HDBC.Sqlite3
```

So, we have imported `Graphics.EasyPlot`, `Database.HDBC`, and `Database.HDBC.Sqlite3`. Two of those imports we've seen from our discussion on the SQLite3 database. The first import, `Graphics.EasyPlot`, is the one that we are introducing in this section. Let's make a connection to our database, as shown in the following screenshot:

```
In [2]: db <- connectSqlite3 "../data/stocks.sqlite3"
```

Now, what we would like to do is our first plot of the Apple adjusted close. So, let's pull out the raw adjusted close data for Apple, as shown in the following screenshot:

```
In [3]: aaplRaw <- quickQuery db "SELECT adjclose FROM aapl" []
```

We are going to call this `aaplRaw`. We are going to ask our database for all of the adjusted close. We will name our column `adjclose` in our Apple table, and now we need to convert this data to the Double type, as shown in the following screenshot:

```
In [4]: :t aaplRaw
        aaplRaw :: [[SqlValue]]
```

You can see that `aaplRaw` is a two-dimensional array of SQL values, and we need to convert this to a single-dimensional array of the Double type. So, let's do that, as shown in the following screenshot.

```
In [5]: aapl = map (fromSql . head) aaplRaw :: [Double]
```

We have mapped `fromSql . head`. It's only going to be a two-dimensional array with one column, so we can just call head on that one column to get the value. We'll convert that into a `Double` type. Let's look at those values that we're going to plot. This is a new command, as follows:

```
In [12]: plot X11 $ zip [0,-1..] aapl
         True
```

X11 means that we're going to plot directly to the X11 Windows environment, and `plot` requires that we have two coordinates: x values and y values. `plot` also requires that we have a list of tuples, where each tuple consists of an x value and a y value. So, we have zipped together our x values, which are simply going to be 0, -1, on to infinity.

The reason why we're using negative values is because our dataset is in reverse chronological order. And then, our y values are going to be the adjusted close data. So, it's going to take a moment to show the following plotting diagram:

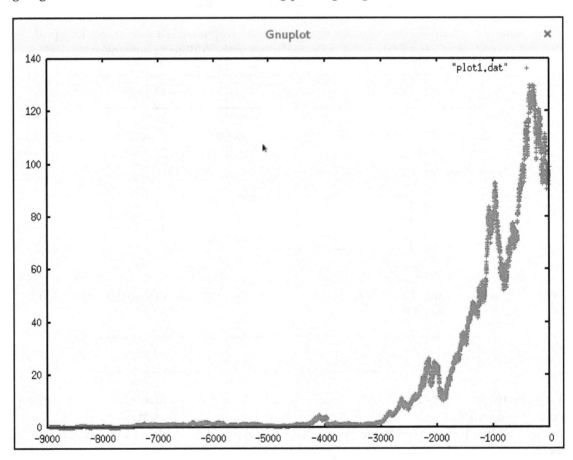

You'll notice a few things. This is not a true line plot. This is a scatter plot with lots of + signs for all of our data points. For most of Apple's history, going back 9,000 trading days, the adjusted close has been less than $20; and it's only been within the last, say, 3,000 trading days that we've seen an increase in the adjusted close share price.

In our next few sections, we're going to talk about how we can clean this image up and make it publication-ready. We're going to be talking about moving averages, and we're going to be talking about feature rescaling. Our next section is going to be all about the moving averages.

Plotting a moving average

We're going to be expanding on our knowledge of average by introducing the moving average. The moving average is simply the average of a subset of the data, where we have a small window in which we compute the average and then we move that window, and then we compute the average again. We keep repeating this until we've expended our data. So, in this section, we're going to take a look at creating line plots. We're going to introduce the moving average, and then we're going to plot a moving average. Let's go back to our notebook and continue from where we left off.

In the last section, the plot that we saw had a lot of + signs, and that doesn't make for an elegant graph. So, what we're going to do is to use a line plot, as demonstrated in the following example:

```
In [13]:  plot X11 $ Data2D [Style Lines] [] (zip [0,-1..] aapl)
          True
```

Now, `Data2D` is the formal way of introducing data to plot. There is the default which we used in the last section, but this is the formal way, which allows for a little more customization. After `Data2D`, you pass in parameters. The first is a list of options, `Style Lines`.

There is a second set of options which you can include after that, but we're going to leave that as a blank list. Finally, we put in our data, (zip [0, -1,..] aapl). This should produce the following line plot:

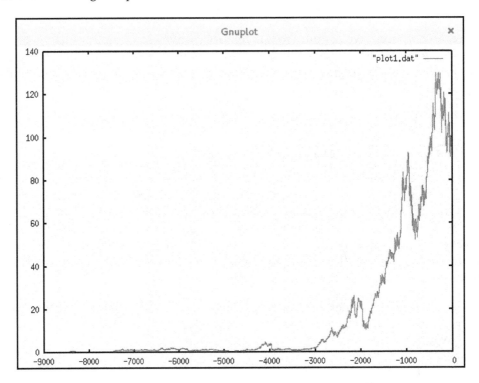

So, here's our line plot, uses a continuous line from start to finish. Notice how jagged it is. That's because this is a real-world dataset, and a real-world dataset is frequently messy. So, this is partly why we're introducing a moving average. What we're going to do now is introduce that moving average. Moving averages are used frequently in the analysis of a stock. For example, it's common for investors to compare a company's 50-day moving average to the 200-day moving average. As this is not a chapter on investing, we're not going to get into the details of interpreting 50- and 200-day moving averages; however, you can research those on your own. In our case, we're going to demonstrate here how to compute a 200-day moving average. These are called 200-day MAs, where MA stands for moving average. So, the first function which we will introduce is known as the movingSum. movingSum is going to compute a list of sums based on the size of a window, and the size of the window is determined by the length of the first list passed to it, as demonstrated in the following screenshot:

```
In [14]:  movingSum :: [Double] -> [Double] -> [Double]
          movingSum xs [] = [sum xs]
          movingSum (x:xs) (y:ys) = (sum (x:xs)):movingSum (xs++[y]) ys
```

You'll see here, in the first line, that there are two parameters being passed to the function: a list of Doubles and a list of Doubles. The first list represents the window which we are trying to sum. The second list represents the rest of the dataset. In the next line, we are saying, if there is no rest of the dataset in our first pattern, then we're just going to return a list containing the sum of the first list. But let's say that there is data in both lists. So, in the third line, you'll see that in the first list we shaved the first value off the first list, and then we computed the sum where we immediately reattached that value onto the list. We then recursively call movingSum again, where we take that first list (from which the first value has been shaved off) and then we add to the end the first value of the second list. Next, we pass the shorter version of the second list as the second parameter. As you can see, the size of the first list always stays the same. So, if the size of the first list is 3 in length, then at the end of the list it will still be 3 in length. So, let's do a quick example of how this works. If we wish to compute the moving sum of the values 1 to 10 but we have a window size of 3, then we need to set our first parameter to be 1,2,3, as shown in the following screenshot:

```
In [15]:  movingSum [1,2,3] [4,5,6,7,8,9,10]

          [6.0,9.0,12.0,15.0,18.0,21.0,24.0,27.0]
```

So, as you can see, we have the moving sum of the values from 1 to 10, but with a window size of 3. So, the sum of 1, 2 and 3 is 6; 2, 3 and 4 is 9; 3, 4 and 5 is 12; 4, 5 and 6 is 15; and so forth, all the way to the end of the list.

Now, our next function is the movingAverage function, and you can see it's longer than our movingSum, but most of this is error checking and looking for data which we should be catching, as shown in the following screenshot:

```
In [16]:  movingAverage :: [Double] -> Int -> [Double]
          movingAverage xs windowSize
            | windowSize < 1 = error "Cannot have non-positive window size."
            | windowSize > length xs = []
            | otherwise = map (/ fromIntegral windowSize) movingSums
            where
              movingSums = movingSum (take windowSize xs) (drop windowSize xs)
```

So, this function is going to take two parameters: our dataset, and then the size of the window that we want. It then passes that information on to movingSum, figures out the moving sums, and then simply divides by the window size for that particular dataset. So, we can find the moving average by using the following command:

```
In [17]: movingAverage [1..10] 3
         [2.0,3.0,4.0,5.0,6.0,7.0,8.0,9.0]
```

We are computing the moving average for our values from 1 to 10 with a window size of 3. So, you can see that 6 divided by 3 is 2; 9 divided by 3 is 3; 27 divided by 3 is 9; and that's all we're doing. If we wish to compute the moving average of our Apple data, we can run the following command:

```
In [18]: aaplMA = movingAverage aapl 200
```

If we want a 200-day moving average, we can just say 200. Now we can plot that dataset as follows:

```
In [21]: plot X11 $ Data2D [Style Lines] [] (zip [0,-1..] aaplMA)
         True
```

This command is similar to what we did earlier and we get the following output:

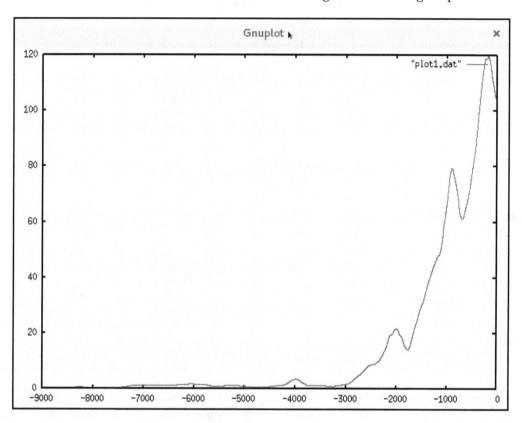

There we go. Remember how jagged the original dataset was? Looking at the plotting of this particular dataset, we can see how smooth it is by comparison. Moving averages will smooth the dataset. It will take the noise and kind of cover it up, and still retain most of the shape of the original dataset. In our next section, we're going to talk about how we can get publication-ready graphs.

Creating publication-ready plots

Creating plots that are publication-ready is essential, simply because we must be able to share our knowledge. In this section, we're going to take a look at plotting multiple variables on a single plot, adding a legend to that plot, and then saving our plots to a file. Let's go back to our notebook and check the last plot that we created in the previous section, which was the 200-day moving average of the stock price of Apple since the beginning. I want to point out a few things about our previous plot. First, we have a legend at the top that just says `plot1.dat`, and, if you've never seen this before, currently that doesn't really mean anything to anyone. Also, there's no way in this mechanism to save to a file the output that you see. We could definitely get some screenshot software and then create our own screenshot of this image, but that'd be a little bit of extra work. Let's go ahead and check out a few customizations of this plot and we would like to save this plot to a file. There are two variables in this notebook that we will be working on. One is `aapl`, which we created in the *Line plots of a single variable* section, and the other one is `aaplMA`, which we created in the *Plotting a moving average* section. What we will do now is plot these two datasets on the same image. To do that we're going to plot X11, and then we're going to introduce a list where each item in that list is going to be Data2D, as demonstrated in the following command:

```
In [22]: plot X11 [Data2D [Style Lines] [] (zip [0,-1..] aapl), Data2D [Style Lines] [] (zip [0,-1..] aaplMA)]
         True
```

As you can see, we have added both the entries here, `aapl` and `aaplMA`. So, that's what our command looks like, and you'll see, from the following screenshot, that we now have two plots on this particular line:

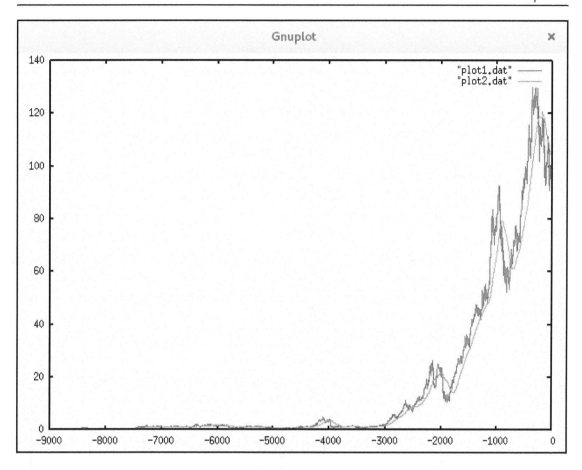

The red line is `aapl` and the green line is `aaplMA`. We have both our original and our moving average plotted on the same plot, and that's nice. Notice how little information is presented from about **-3000** to **-9000**. It's almost a straight line. There's a little bump there at **-4000**, but the most interesting parts of the data are within the last 2,000 trading days. So, let's go ahead and plot just the last 2,000 trading days. So, we are going to modify our last statement as follows:

```
In [23]: plot X11
           [ Data2D [Style Lines] [] (zip [0,-1..] (take 2000 aapl))
           , Data2D [Style Lines] [] (zip [0,-1..] (take 2000 aaplMA))
           ]
         True
```

In our dataset, we have added `take 2000` and this is going to plot just the last 2,000 trading days, as demonstrated in the following screenshot:

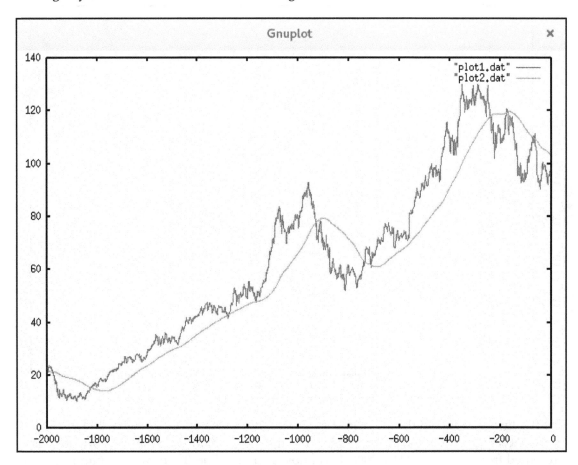

So, take a moment, and examine that green line. Do you notice something funny about it? It's supposed to be a moving average, but if it were a true moving average, shouldn't it follow the red line more closely? It looks like it's lagging behind the red line a little bit. That's because the moving average is always computing the previous 200 data points. We would really like to center that moving average over the point where it spreads 100 units in either direction. So, we can make a quick change to our plot, where we simply reset the starting point of the moving average to be 100 points behind, as shown in the following command:

```
In [*]: plot X11
         [ Data2D [Style Lines] [] (zip [0,-1..] (take 2000 aapl))
         , Data2D [Style Lines] [] (zip [-100,-101..] (take 2000 aaplMA))
         ]
        True
```

So, for dataset `aaplMA`, we'll start the list with −100 and −101. We're starting at −100 simply because 100 is half of 200. This achieves the following result:

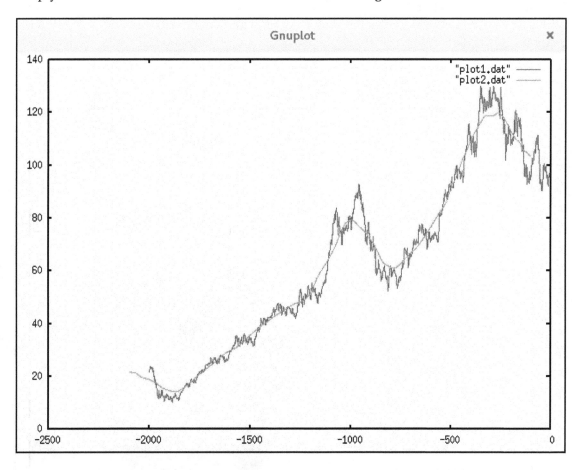

This plot has a much better moving average, where the green line now delicately hugs that red line. It's a much better visualization. Now, imagine that you're seeing this image for the first time and you have no idea what these lines mean, and there is a legend in this plot but it just says **plot1.dat** and plot2.dat.

Those aren't helpful at all. What we need to do now is introduce titles to each of these plots. So we are again going to modify our statement, as demonstrated in the following example:

```
In [25]: plot X11
            [ Data2D [Style Lines, Title "AAPL Adj. Close"] [] (zip [0,-1..] (take 2000 aapl))
            , Data2D [Style Lines, Title "AAPL 200-day MA"] [] (zip [-100,-101..] (take 2000 aaplMA))
            ]
         True
```

Now in the options, after `Style Lines`, we have the option of creating a title, so we have added `AAPL Adj. Close` and `AAPL 220-day MA`. This is demonstrated with the following graph:

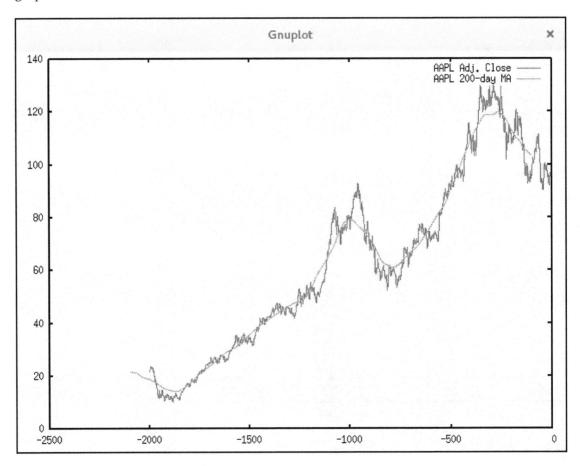

Now you can quickly identify a line based on its color, and you can see which color is associated with each dataset. This is important for the sharing of knowledge. Let's say that we don't like the colors of our plot. Our defaults are red and green, and that's great for most cases, but let's change this to, say, blue and black. We will take our plot again, and, after our title, we will add the colors as follows:

```
In [26]: plot X11
           [ Data2D [Style Lines, Title "AAPL Adj. Close", Color Blue] [] (zip [0,-1..] (take 2000 aapl))
           , Data2D [Style Lines, Title "AAPL 200-day MA", Color Black] [] (zip [-100,-101..] (take 2000 aaplMA))
           ]
         True
```

The result with new colors is as follows:

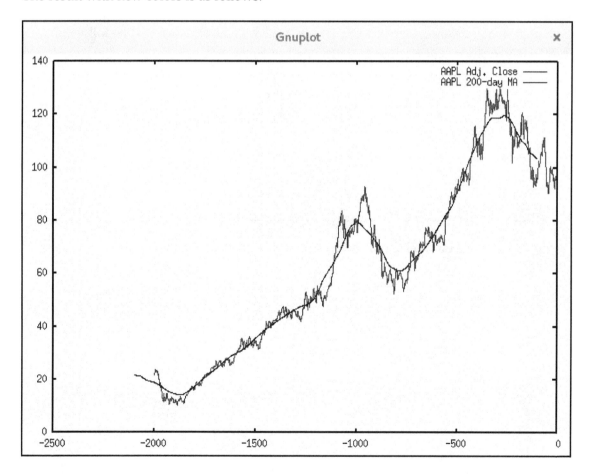

Now, if you go through the EasyPlot documentation, you're going to see lots of colors that can be defined for our plots. Finally, we would like to save this plot. To do that, we need to change how the image is directed, and that involves changing X11, as demonstrated in the following command:

```
In [27]:  plot (PNG "adjcloseWith200DayMA.png")
            [ Data2D [Style Lines, Title "AAPL Adj. Close", Color Blue] [] (zip [0,-1..] (take 2000 aapl))
            , Data2D [Style Lines, Title "AAPL 200-day MA", Color Black] [] (zip [-100,-101..] (take 2000 aaplMA))
            ]
          True
```

So, we have changed X11 to PNG, which means we are saving this as a PNG file. We have named the file adjcloseWith20DayMA.png. Now, it doesn't display anything on the screen. It simply writes that to a file in our local directory. If we go to our Terminal, and look at our analysis folder, we will see the file present there, as shown by the following screenshot:

```
jcchurch@dataanalysis:~/Code/HaskellDataAnalysis/analysis$ ls
adjcloseWith200DayMA.png   Earthquakes-Connect.ipynb
Baseball.ipynb             Earthquakes.ipynb
Baseball-Mean.ipynb        Earthquakes-SELECT.ipynb
Baseball-Median.ipynb      plot1.dat
Baseball-Mode.ipynb        plot2.dat
Baseball-OpenCSV.ipynb     StockAnalysis-FirstPlot.ipynb
Baseball-Range.ipynb       StockAnalysis.ipynb
DescriptiveStats.hs        StockAnalysis-MovingAverage.ipynb
jcchurch@dataanalysis:~/Code/HaskellDataAnalysis/analysis$ iceweasel adjcloseWit
h200DayMA.png
```

Next, I have used Iceweasel to look at my file. The output will be shown on a browser as follows:

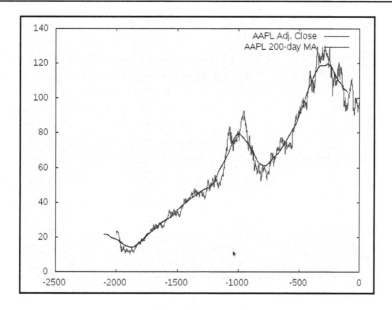

Great. Now we can drop that image into a publication—say, a Word document or a LaTeX document and it should be sufficient. Now, one thing that `EasyPlot` won't do is that it won't add titles and it won't add axis lines. So, what I recommend you to do is add that information into the legend details. In our next section we will looking at feature rescaling.

Feature scaling

In our last section, we explored the essential features of `EasyPlot` towards getting our images publication-ready. In this section, we're going to explore how to plot multiple companies onto a single plot to accurately reflect their growth. So, the question we would like to answer in this section is: over the past year, which of these three companies—Apple, Google, or Microsoft—has had the highest percentage of growth in their stock value? In this section, we're going to take a look at trimming our dataset to 252 days. Why 252? Well, there are 365 days in the year. If you cut out the weekends and the United States federal holidays in which the New York Stock Exchange doesn't operate, you're left with 252 days. So, 252 is our magic number to represent one year of trading data. We're going to introduce feature scaling, and we're going to plot our three companies that have been feature scaled. So, here's the formula for feature scaling:

$$\frac{x - X_1}{max(X) - min(X)}$$

It is simply a value, minus the first value in our dataset, divided by the difference between the largest and smallest values. It's a fairly simple formula, and what this formula does is take any dataset and rescale it so that it's on the range of -1 to 1. What's also nice about feature scaling is that this formula won't change the shape of your data at all. The shape remains the same. Now, let's go over to our notebook and fetch out the Microsoft and Google datasets from our database. As mentioned at the start of this chapter, I would like you to build a database of three different companies, and I hope you have that datasets ready. If not, I hope you're willing to grab the dataset that accompanies this chapter, as shown in the following screenshot, so that you can follow along:

```
In [36]:
        googlRaw <- quickQuery db "SELECT adjclose FROM googl" []
        msftRaw <- quickQuery db "SELECT adjclose FROM msft" []
        googl = map (fromSql . head) googlRaw :: [Double]
        msft = map (fromSql . head) msftRaw :: [Double]
```

Now here, we have the lines ready to go in order to pool our Google and Microsoft datasets. Google's stock symbol is known as GOOGL, and so we have named our table `googl`, and Microsoft's stock symbol is MSFT, therefore we have named our table `msft`. What we need to do next is to trim our datasets to the most recent 252 trading days, as demonstrated in the following screenshot:

```
In [37]:  aapl252 = take 252 aapl

In [38]:  msft252 = take 252 msft

In [39]:  googl252 = take 252 googl
```

We have called all of these datasets by their symbol followed by the number 252. So, we have taken 252 from `aapl252`, `msft252`, and `googl252`. Next, we would like to plot these datasets so that you can get an idea of what they look like in their original shape on scale, as shown in the following example:

```
In [40]: plot X11
           [ Data2D [Style Lines, Title "AAPL"] [] (zip [0,-1..] aapl252)
           , Data2D [Style Lines, Title "MSFT"] [] (zip [0,-1..] msft252)
           , Data2D [Style Lines, Title "GOOGL"] [] (zip [0,-1..] googl252)
           ]
         True
```

The first dataset on the following example will be Apple, the second will be Microsoft, and the third will be Google:

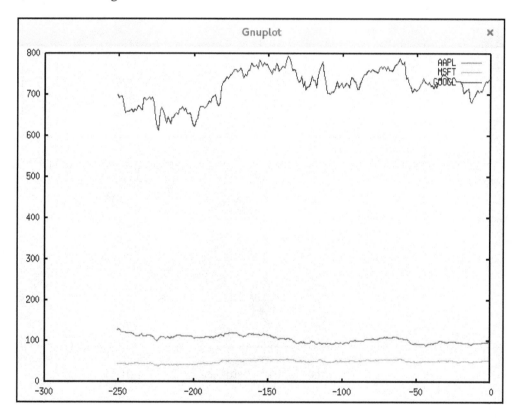

It'll just be the most recent 252 trading days. Each of these three companies trades at a particular dollar value, but each of them trades at a dollar value that doesn't relate to any of the other companies; and this is true for any stock that's publicly traded on the stock market. If you know the price of a company, that really doesn't tell you anything about if that company is doing well or not. We would like to feature scale these three companies so that they all exist on the same plot and they all exist at the same scale. So, let's introduce our feature scale function. So, our feature scale function, which is shown in the following example, is going to be called `rescale`:

```
In [41]:
        rescale :: [Double] -> [Double]
        rescale xs = map (\x -> (x - lead)/(diffxs)) xs
          where
            lead = last xs
            maxxs = maximum xs
            minxs = minimum xs
            diffxs = maxxs - minxs
```

It is an implementation of the formula that we saw at the start of this section, and it takes one dataset and it returns a dataset of equal length. As you will see, the shape of these datasets will remain the same but the scale of the datasets will be on the range of -1 to 1, as shown in the following example:

```
In [26]: plot X11
            [ Data2D [Style Lines, Title "AAPL"] [] (zip [0,-1..] (rescale aapl252))
            , Data2D [Style Lines, Title "MSFT"] [] (zip [0,-1..] (rescale msft252))
            , Data2D [Style Lines, Title "GOOGL"] [] (zip [0,-1..] (rescale googl252))
            ]
         True
```

So, we have rescaled each of our three datasets using `rescale` in our plot line, and our plot is shown in the following screenshot:

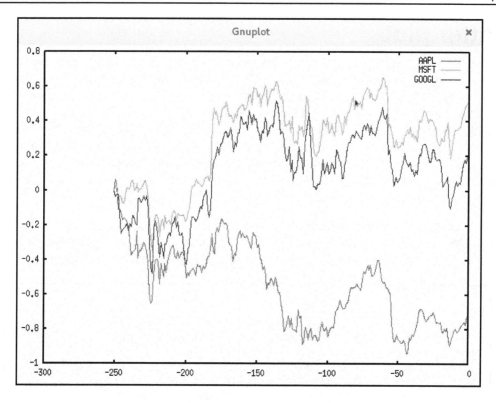

Now, notice that because every data point is first subtracted by the very first element, the very first element for all three lists should be 0, and you can see that that's true in the previous plot. So, this is the feature scale plot for all three of our datasets. We can tell that the green line corresponds to the company that has grown the most, the blue line has corresponded to the company that has grown the second most, and the red line corresponds to the company that has grown the least. And, in order, it looks like the green line is Microsoft, the blue line is Google, and the red line is Apple. So, over the past year, Microsoft has done the best and Apple has done the least well. We can also tell from this particular plot that Microsoft and Google have increased in value over the past year, whereas Apple appears to have decreased in value over the past year.

Feature scaling allows us to take any companies and plot them on the same chart, and allows us to accurately compare the values of those companies without losing the original shape of the lines produced by their values. In our next section, we will cover scatter plots.

Scatter plots

The financial data that we've used up to this point in this section is usually considered time series data. Time series data is simply sequential data that usually includes a date or a timestamp. Scatter plots don't have to be tied to sequential data. So, in this section, what we would like to do is develop an understanding of the share price of a stock, and how much that stock is traded in terms of volume. So, we're going to be comparing the stock price to the volume traded, with a relatively simple plot. You're going to see very quickly that this plot is insufficient to meet our needs of understanding the plot. So, we're going to be comparing that stock price with the log of the volume traded. So, what we would like to do in this section is to perform this analysis on Apple, Google, and Microsoft.

Let's go back to our notebook where we can see our stock analysis. We already have the adjusted close values for Apple, Microsoft, and Google; and what we need now is simply to get the raw data for the volume, as demonstrated in the following screenshot:

```
In [27]:
        aaplVolRaw <- quickQuery db "SELECT volume FROM aapl" []
        msftVolRaw <- quickQuery db "SELECT volume FROM msft" []
        googlVolRaw <- quickQuery db "SELECT volume FROM googl" []
        aaplVol = map (fromSql . head) aaplVolRaw :: [Double]
        msftVol = map (fromSql . head) msftVolRaw :: [Double]
        googlVol = map (fromSql . head) googlVolRaw :: [Double]
```

We are pulling the volume data out of our database in much the same way as we pulled the adjusted close. So, let's go ahead and run it. Our adjusted close values are all the symbol itself for the three respective companies, whereas the volume is going to be the symbol plus the word Vol, as you can see in these last three lines. If we plot that adjust to close we will see the following code:

```
In [28]:  plot X11 $ zip aapl aaplVol

          True
```

So, we're going to be comparing AAPL with AAPL's volume, as shown in the following graph:

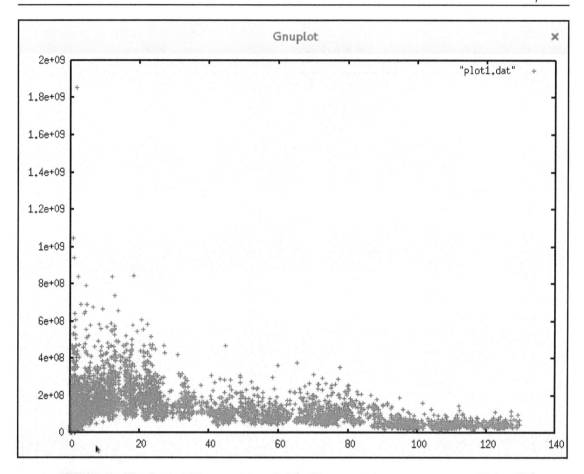

Now, what you're looking at here is that, along the x axis, we have the share price of the company, and, along the y axis, which stretches into - I believe that's in billions—we have the volume traded. You can see that there's a huge shift on the left side of the graph, there are lots and lots of data points; whereas, on the right side of the graph, there's not much. And we have one lone dot way up that is extending our plot. This doesn't really give you a good idea about the shape of the data. So, in order to solve this, we can compress the data near the top while doing relatively little to the data at the bottom. There's a simple math expression for this, where you simply take the log of the plot. So, let's go ahead and apply that log to our volume data, as shown in the following example:

```
In [29]: plot X11 $ zip aapl (map log aaplVol)
         True
```

So, we have used `map log` on volume. So, as you can see in the following graph, taking a log of the volume data does change the shape:

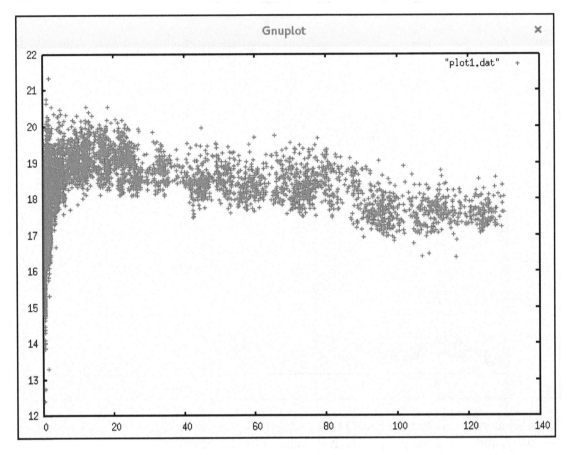

Unlike our past section, where we tried to retain the shape of the data, taking the log of the plot loses a lot of the shape of that data, but this also allows us to focus in on those lower values. So, here you can see an obvious trend line that's downward so that, as the stock price increases, the volume traded decreases. Before the stock price of 20 or maybe even 10, it doesn't seem to even really matter. But after 10, you can see a noticeable drop that seems to have a pattern to it. Now, this is just for Apple's stock price. What we would like to do is see if this holds up true for our other companies. So, let's plot all three of our companies, with a log plot, as shown in the following example:

```
In [*]: plot X11 [ Data2D [Title "AAPL"] [] (zip aapl (map log aaplVol))
                 , Data2D [Title "MSFT"] [] (zip msft (map log msftVol))
                 , Data2D [Title "GOOGL"] [] (zip googl (map log googlVol))
                 ]
```

This is not going to be an accurate reflection of the three companies combined because, as we have already said, the log plot does change the shape of the data. What I would mostly like you to do, whenever we run this plot, is to examine the trends of each of the three companies. Notice that all we're doing is taking a log of the volume for the respective companies, as shown in the following graph:

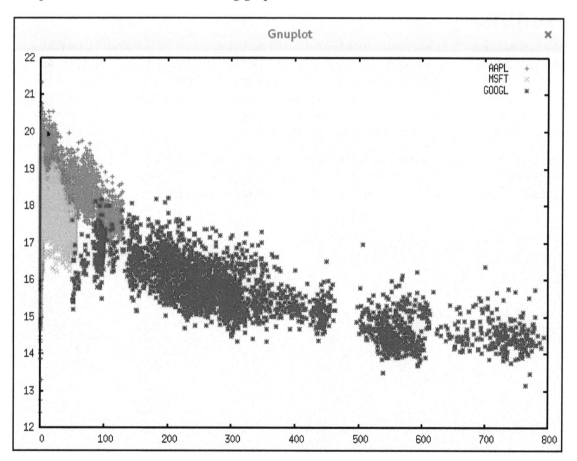

Here we have, in red, the original Apple dataset which you saw earlier. In green, we have the Microsoft dataset; and, in blue, we have the Google dataset. You'll notice that all three datasets have that downward trend. We wouldn't have been able to see that downward trend without taking a log of the data. So, why do we see this downward trend? Well, there's a relatively simple explanation. As companies increase in value, our purchasing power decreases and we can buy fewer shares. We're highlighting the advantages to the adage of buy low, sell high. There's not a lot of predictive analytic power to this particular visualization, but I still believe that there's an educational value to it.

Summary

We began the section with installing the `gnuplot` and the `EasyPlot` Haskell library. We discussed the moving average using the 200-day and the 50-day moving average, which is frequently used by analysts in market analysis. But beware, these are not substitutions for good, solid research. We discussed how to make our plots publication-ready by adding a legend and saving our images to files, and we discussed how to feature scale our plot so that it's on the range of -1 to 1. Feature scaling always retains the shape of the data.

Finally, we demonstrated the utility of taking the log of data. It allowed us to compress higher values, while retaining the general shape of lower values. This changes the overall shape of a plot. In our next chapter, we will discuss the normal distribution.

Kernel Density Estimation

5

In this chapter, we are going to cover kernel density estimation. Since kernel density estimation is a rather involved operation, we're going to split this up over several sections so hopefully it's easier to digest.

In this chapter, we are going to cover the following topics:

- Introducing the central limit theorem
- Introducing normal distribution
- Introducing the kernel density estimator
- Applying the kernel density estimator to a dataset

The central limit theorem

In this section, we'll be discussing the central limit theorem, which is essential to our understanding of normal distribution. Normal distribution is an important formula for the study of even basic statistics in data science. Data science, at its heart, is mathematical. We're transitioning away from the technical aspects of Haskell and file formats. First let's look at the central limit theorem before we introduce normal distribution, and then we're going to be exploring the parameters of normal distribution. So, here is the definition of the central limit theorem as per Wikipedia:

> *The central limit theorem (CLT) states that, given certain conditions, the arithmetic mean of a sufficiently large number of iterates of independent random variables, each with a well-defined (finite) expected value and finite variance, will be approximately normally distributed, regardless of the underlying distribution.*

Now, I realize that's a mouthful, but let's see if I can convert this definition into some plain English. Imagine that you have a large data source, and we've worked with several datasets that are sufficiently large, and need to calculate the mean and the standard deviation. You can't, it won't work. We're going to split that data into smaller chunks. We're going to take the averages of each of those smaller chunks.

We're going to count how many times we see each average, and then we're going to plot that information. Once you get that plot, you'll always get something that looks like normal distribution; and this happens regardless of whatever your original data source is. Now let's go over to our Jupyter Notebook and create a notebook entitled Normal, and we have a few imports ready to go, as the following screenshot shows:

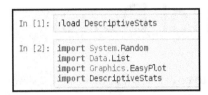

The one import that we're using here that you may not be familiar with is System.Random, and that is for generating random numbers. So, to begin, we need to create our random number generator, as shown in the following example:

```
In [3]: g <- newStdGen
```

This is what we're going to use in order to demonstrate the random number generator. Next, we will generate 100,000 values, in the range of 1 to 100, as the following example shows:

```
In [5]: values = take 100000 (randomRs (1,100) g) :: [Double]
```

We have used a function called randomRs that generates an infinite stream of random number variables, and we're going to take the first 100,000 from that list. So, randomRs, generates our random stream on our range from 1 to 100. You then have to pass in the random number generator, g, which we defined earlier, and we're going to specify that these values are all going to be Double. The first 10 values in our list should look like the following screenshot:

```
In [6]: take 10 values
        [58.78013806951732,3.050543072227301,29.024389411225123,85.73139042381948,69.36536178205485,99.0783590607034,58.173483315
        06121,87.13442820846359,54.61911359384984,25.05354227810114]
```

You can see that they're all Double, they have long floating-point portions, and they're the first 10 values. What we need to do now is to divide this dataset up into chunks, and for that we would generate 10,000 chunks, each of size 10. So, let's create our quick function, as demonstrated in the following example:

```
In [7]: chunk [] = []
        chunk list = take 10 list : chunk (drop 10 list)
```

This function is called `chunk`, and, if it takes an empty list it'll just return an empty list, but, if it sees a list with data in it, it's going to take the first 10 items of that list and then recursively call itself by dropping those first 10 items and passing the remainder. So, this is going to generate our list, where each sublist will be 10 elements long. Now, let's check out the length of `chunkedValues`, as demonstrated in the following example:

```
In [8]: chunkedValues = chunk values

In [9]: length chunkedValues
        10000
```

We have 10,000, which is what we were expecting: 10,000 times 10 is 100,000, which is our original value. Next, we need to compute the average of each of these chunks, as shown in the following example:

```
In [10]: avgs = map (\xs -> sum xs / genericLength xs) chunkedValues
```

We have taken the average of each of these sublists, so we now need to record how often we notice each average. To do this, we are going to cheat a little bit—only a little—and round this information to the nearest integer. We then sort the lists of values and perform run-length encoding, which we generated back in Chapter 1, *Descriptive Statistics*. This is shown in the following screenshot:

```
In [11]: pairs = runLengthEncoding $ sort (map round avgs)
```

So, `pairs` is going to be equal to `runLengthEncoding`, and we're going to pass in our sorted map, where we round each of our averages. Now, let's plot to the screen, as shown in the following example:

```
In [12]: plot X11 $ Data2D [Style Lines] [] (map (\(x,y) -> (fromIntegral x, y)) pairs)
         Use first
         Found:                            Why Not:
           \ (x, y) -> (fromIntegral x, y)  Control.Arrow.first fromIntegral
         True
```

We're going to map our values over this quick little function, `map`. You're going to see why we did this in a little bit. Since our run-length encoding algorithm produces an integral value for each of the first values in our list, the plot function doesn't know how to plot that. So, we have to convert from integral. Thus we have used `fromIntegral` on our x, and then we passed in our y, and then we passed in our `pairs`. Since this is a randomly generated dataset, we don't know what's going to be displayed. An example is shown in the following screenshot:

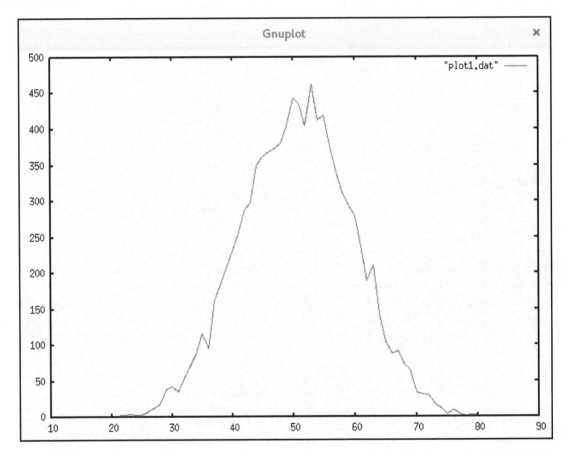

Now, according to the central limit theorem, whatever is displayed should be approximately normal distribution. The characteristics of normal distribution are that it has a high center in the middle, and extends downward pretty evenly on both sides; and so here we have that approximated normal distribution. Looking at the approximated normal distribution, you will see that it's jagged, because our data is random and not perfect. What we would like to do now is to introduce the actual normal distribution.

Normal distribution

In this section, we are going to see normal distribution. The formula for normal distribution is as follows:

$$f(x; \mu, \sigma) = \frac{1}{\sqrt{2\sigma^2\pi}} e^{-\frac{(x-\mu)^2}{2\sigma^2}}$$

I realize this formula is intense if you've never seen it before, but focus in on the parameter side instead of the actual formula side. There are only three parameters: x, μ and σ. x is the dataset, which represents the domain; μ represents the mean, where we want the mean of our dataset to be; and σ represents the standard deviation, or how thin or wide we want our dataset to be. Now, because this is a hairy formula I've already implemented it, and I'm going to paste it into our window. So, the following example shows our quick function for normal distribution, where you can see the three parameters:

```
In [13]:  normal mu sd x = exp (-((x-mu)^2 / (2*sd*sd))) / sqrt (2*sd*sd*pi)
```

We have mu, which represents the mean; sd, which represents the standard deviation; and x, which is the domain over which we are mapping. Now, here's what you need to remember about the two parameters, the two key parameters mu and sd: mu represents the centerline location. Positive means it'll exist to the right of 0 and negative means it'll exist to the left of 0. The standard deviation, sd, represents the width. High numbers in the standard deviation represent wide plots that are low, and low numbers in standard deviation represent high plots which are thin and narrow. So, let's go ahead and plot our normal distribution. We need to plot over the domain, and I prefer to plot on the domain of −5 in 1/10 increments, as shown in the following example:

```
In [14]:  domain = [-5,-4.9,.5]
```

Now, let's plot our values, as can be seen in the following example:

```
In [15]:  plot X11 $ Data2D [Style Lines] [] (zip domain (map (normal 0 1) domain))
          True
```

We have zipped our domain and mapped which domain over the normal distribution. We have specified a mean of 0 and a standard deviation of 1. Then we have mapped our domain over that normal formula, as shown in the following graph:

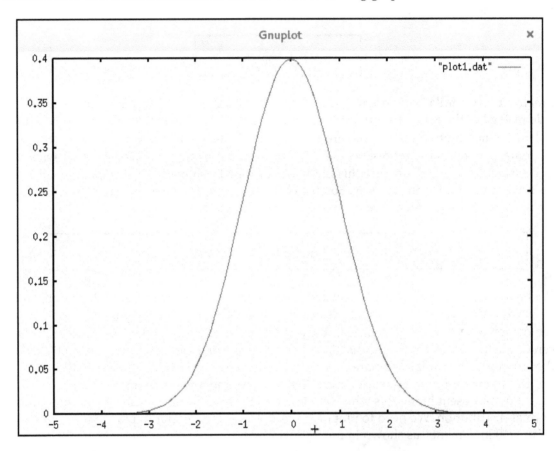

So, what you see in the previous graph is the true normal distribution. You can see that the peak of the normal distribution is at 0.4, and the width of the normal distribution extends just past -3 on the left and 3 on the right. Take a mental note of those values, where at 0 our peak is at 0.4 and our widths are at -3 and 3. We're going to come back to those values.

Now let's continue to demonstrate how the standard deviation affects these parameters. Look at the following example:

```
In [16]:  plot X11 $ Data2D [Style Lines] [] (zip domain (map (normal 0 5) domain))
          True
```

We have changed the standard deviation to 5. Large standard deviations produce wide plots that are low, as shown in the following graph:

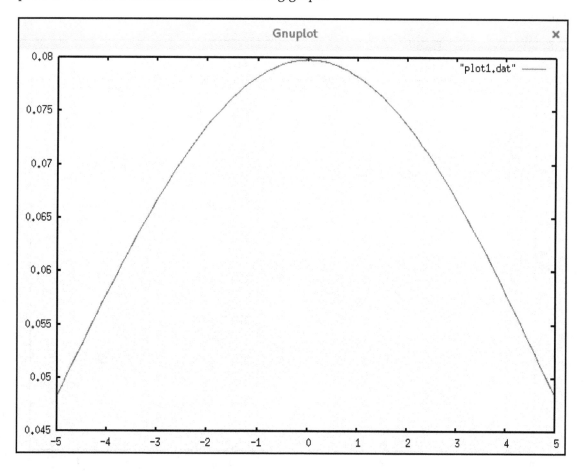

The peak of our standard deviation is still over 0 because our mean is at 0, but now it's only at 0.08. Our widths extend well beyond −5 and 5. So, this is a much wider plot that's lower. Let's perform this again, by changing the standard deviation to 0.5, as shown in the following example:

```
In [17]: plot X11 $ Data2D [Style Lines] [] (zip domain (map (normal 0 0.5) domain))
         True
```

We should get the following output:

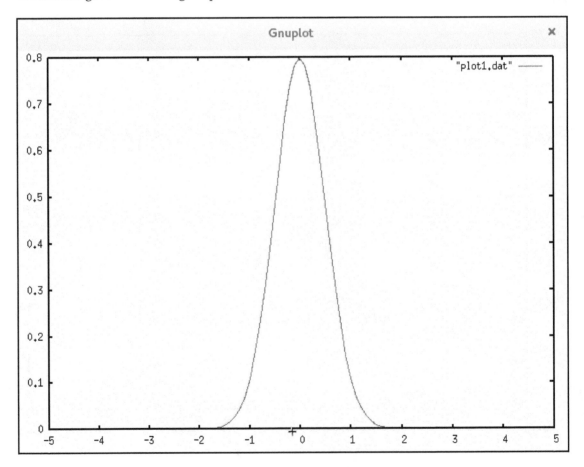

Once again we're over 0, and we have a much narrower plot that only exists from between −2 and −1; and, on the other side, between 1 and 2. The peak of our plot is now at 0.8, so it's much higher than our original. Now that we've seen how standard deviation affects the plot, let's see how the mean affects the plot. To do this, we are going to go back to our original statement with a standard deviation of 1 and a mean of 0, and we are going to change the mean to 2, as shown in the following example:

```
In [18]: plot X11 $ Data2D [Style Lines] [] (zip domain (map (normal 2 1) domain))
         True
```

Let's look at the output now:

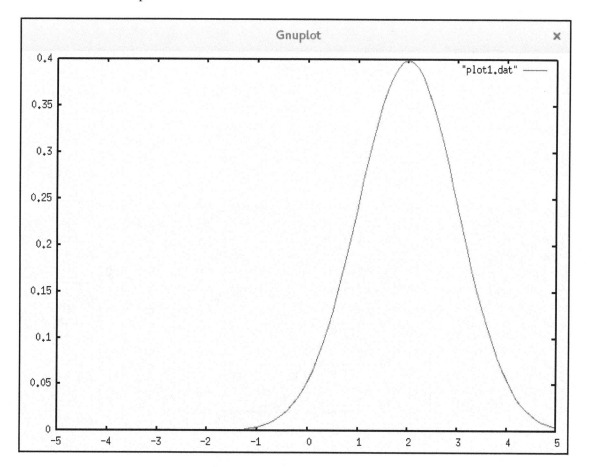

So, whenever you have two standard deviations which are the same, the shape of the data will be identical, just the mean offset will be different. Before, we had a mean of 0 and the center of the plot was over 0; and now we have a mean of 2 and the center of the plot is over 2. Everything else about the plot is the same. The width is the same, and the height is the same. Now that you have a little bit of a background on the central limit theorem and normal distribution, and the two key parameters of normal distribution—the mean and the standard deviation—we're ready to go ahead and talk about kernel density estimation. So, our next section will be about how to implement the kernel density estimator.

Introducing kernel density estimation

Kernel density estimation is a process by which we can estimate the shape of a dataset. After we have computed the shape of a dataset, we can compute the probability in which an event will happen.

In this section, we're going to introduce the kernel density estimator. The kernel density estimator requires a kernel function, and we are going to discuss the requirements of the kernel function and how the normal distribution meets those requirements. Finally, we're going to compute the KDE of a set of values. So, kernel density estimation tries to estimate the shape of a dataset. All data has a shape - we could also refer to this as the density - and that shape is not always clear. Once we have estimated the shape of a dataset, we can compute the probability of a particular observation.

We require a kernel function, and in this section we will use the normal. There are three requirements of a kernel and there are several different types of formulas which meet these requirements. The first is that a kernel needs to be smooth. Secondly, a kernel needs to be symmetrical and non-negative. Symmetrical means that for a given position that is negative, you have the exact same value for the same position when it is positive. Non-negative simply means that the line exists at or above 0. And then, finally, the final requirement is that the area under the curve is 1. So, the following diagram shows the formula for the normal distribution, expressed as an integral from negative infinity to infinity, with a result that should be 1:

$$1 = \int_{-\infty}^{\infty} \frac{1}{\sqrt{2\sigma^2\pi}} e^{-\frac{(x-\mu)^2}{2\sigma^2}} \, dx$$

What's nice about normal distribution is that it doesn't matter what you set as the mean or as the standard deviation, the result will always be 1. So, here's the general algorithm for kernel density estimation. For each value in our dataset, we're going to compute a normal curve with a mean of that value. So, the curve itself is going to shift around. We're going to take all of those curves and we're going to add them together; and then finally, we're going to plot.

So, let's go over to our notebook, and we're going to take a small set of values, only three, as shown in the following example:

```
In [18]: values = [1, 1, 5]
```

We are calling this `values`, and we have passed in `[1, 1, 5]`. Let's imagine that we have a dataset and we're trying to understand the shape of this dataset, but we only have these three values to work with. We can take the range of these values, and by looking at them, you can tell the range is 1 to 5, as shown in the following example:

```
In [19]: range values

         Just (1,5)
```

Now, whenever we compute a kernel density estimation, we need to set a domain. I like to pick my domain to be whatever is 5 minus the lowest, all the way up to 5 greater than the highest. So, we need to set a domain from −4 to −3.9, all the way up to 10, as shown in the following screenshot:

```
In [20]: domain = [-4,-3.9..10]
```

That is a fairly broad domain, and I think this produces nice plots. Our next step is to compute the normal of each of our datasets. So, `curve1` will be the normal at mean 1, because 1 is in our dataset and we will keep the standard deviation at 1, as shown in the following screenshot:

```
In [21]: curve1 = map (normal 1 1) domain
```

curve2 will be our normal at position 5, because that's another one of our values. Again, we will keep the standard deviation at 1,as shown in the following example:

```
In [22]: curve2 = map (normal 5 1) domain
```

So, for each value in our dataset we compute normal, where the mean of normal is at that value's position. So, let's go ahead and create a list of all of our curves, in the following way:

```
In [23]: curves = [curve1, curve1, curve2]
```

Now we need to compute the kernel density estimation, where we will add up all the curves together, as shown in the following example:

```
In [24]: kde = foldl1 (zipWith (+)) curves
```

We have called this as kde, where we have used the tool foldl1. foldl1 is a nice little Haskell power tool for combining a list. We have then used zipwith with a + over our list of curves, and that adds up all of our curve data together. Now let's go ahead and plot this information, to see what it looks like, as shown in the following example:

```
In [25]: plot X11 $ [Data2D [Style Lines] [] (zip domain kde)]
Redundant $
Found:                                                  Why Not:
    plot X11 $ [Data2D [Style Lines] [] (zip domain kde)] plot X11 [Data2D [Style Lines] [] (zip domain kde)]
    True
```

We have zipped our `domain` with our `kde`. The following graph shows the shape of our dataset:

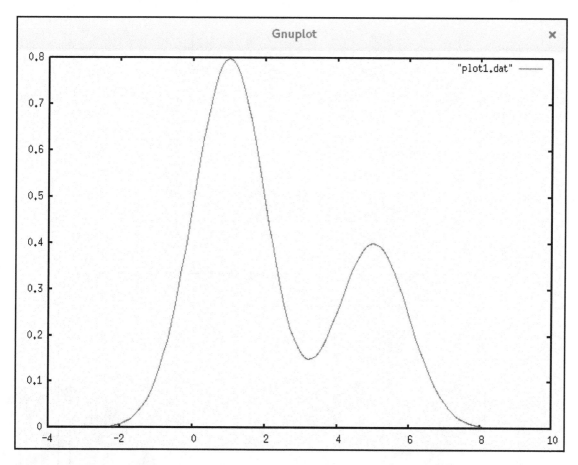

Now, don't try to read too much into the y axis at this point. Just try to notice that, at about position 1, we have a very high likelihood, and, at position 5, we have another high likelihood. There is a dip at position 3, which is midway between 1 and 5. And, also notice, the graph tends to trail off in both directions on either side. So, this is the shape of our `[1, 1, 5]` dataset. Now, what I'd like to do is make the area under this curve equal to 1, and we can do that in the following way:

```
In [26]: kdeAdj = map (/ sum kde) kde
```

We have called it kdeAdj, and we have simply divided it by the sum of the dataset. Now, if we compute the sum of kdeAdj, we will get the following output:

```
In [27]:  sum kdeAdj
          0.9999999999999994
```

We've got a value that's almost 1, and now we are going to plot for kdeAdj, as shown in the following example:

```
In [28]:  plot X11 $ [Data2D [Style Lines] [] (zip domain kdeAdj)]
          Redundant $
          Found:                                              Why Not:
          plot X11 $ [Data2D [Style Lines] [] (zip domain kdeAdj)] plot X11 [Data2D [Style Lines] [] (zip domain kdeAdj)]
          True
```

The output for this would be as follows:

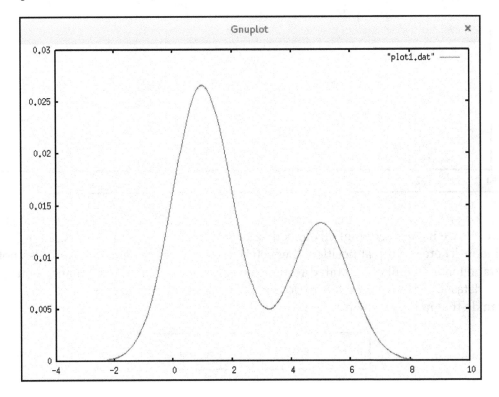

Now, this won't change the shape of our dataset, but it does now introduce probabilities for events. For example, if we assume that we have a continuous dataset, the probability that we will get exactly 1 is a little over 2.5 %; and the probability that we'll see a 5 looks like it's a little less than 1.5 %; and the probability that we'll get a 3 is about a half of a percent. So, notice that the graph is continuous and that we are allowed to see the probability of every point along the shape of our dataset, not just at the integer portions. Alright, we now have enough to introduce the KDE function, which will be introduced at the beginning of the next section. So, in our next section, we're going to introduce an application of the kernel density estimator, along with the kernel density estimator function.

Application of the KDE

This section will serve as our real-world application of the kernel density estimator. In this section, we're going to take a look at the Monet dataset. Monet was a famous French impressionist painter, and many of his paintings have sold at auction for millions of dollars. The Monet dataset is a record of all of those final auction prices for his paintings. We'll be discussing the parts of the kernel density estimator function, and then we will be answering the following question, using the kernel density estimator: what is the probability that, in the future, a Monet painting will sell for 5 million dollars or more? Let's do a Google search for Monet paintings, as illustrated by the following screenshot:

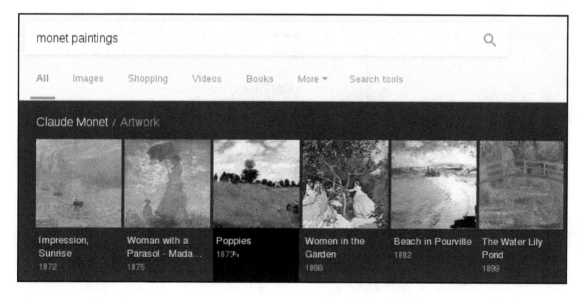

This is my excuse for putting beautiful Monet paintings in our book, and we're going to be discussing the auction prices of these paintings. Aren't those lovely? Hopefully, you have recognized a few of those. Now let's go ahead and find the data set, as demonstrated by the following screenshot:

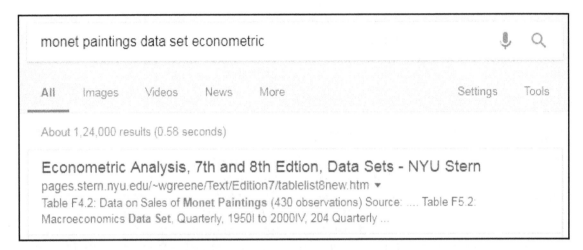

We are looking for the link Econometric Analysis, 7th Edition and 8th Edition, Data Sets. Let's click on it and scroll down to look for the option for Monet datasets, as shown in the next screenshot:

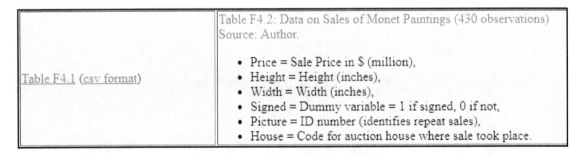

It's **Table F4.1**. There are several columns in this particular dataset but we're only interested in the first one, and that is Sale Price, which is in millions. We're going to download the csv format of the dataset as seen in the above screenshot. Now let's rename the downloaded file TableF4.1.csv to monet.csv, as shown in the following example:

```
jcchurch@dataanalysis:~/Downloads$ ls
aapl.csv          earthquakes.csv   gl2015.zip        usgs.sqlite3
all_week.csv  GL2015.TXT        TableF4-1.csv
jcchurch@dataanalysis:~/Downloads$ mv TableF4-1.csv monet.csv
jcchurch@dataanalysis:~/Downloads$ vi monet.csv █
```

Let's open the file using the command `vi monet.csv:`, as shown in the following code:

```
PRICE,HEIGHT,WIDTH,SIGNED,PICTURE,HOUSE ^M
3.9937800,21.3000000,25.6000000,1,1,1 ^M
8.8000000,31.9000000,25.6000000,1,2,2 ^M
.1316940,6.9000000,15.9000000,0,3,3 ^M
2.0375000,25.7000000,32,1,4,2 ^M
1.4875000,25.7000000,32,1,4,2 ^M
1.8700000,25.6000000,31.9000000,1,4,1 ^M
5.2825000,25.5000000,35.6000000,1,5,1 ^M
5.0657500,26,34.3000000,1,5,2 ^M
1.3750000,25.6000000,36.2000000,1,5,2 ^M
2.5300000,25.6000000,36.4000000,1,6,2 ^M
3.7425000,25.6000000,36.4000000,1,6,2 ^M
.3643430,25.6000000,36.2000000,1,7,2 ^M
2.7238700,31.9000000,39.4000000,1,8,2 ^M
3.5200000,23.6000000,31.9000000,1,9,1 ^M
.4975000,19.5000000,25,1,10,2 ^M
9.3500000,32.7000000,26.8000000,1,11,1 ^M
1.2195000,25.5000000,36,1,12,2 ^M
.4070000,25.6000000,39.4000000,1,12,2 ^M
3.7133900,25.6000000,36.2000000,1,13,3 ^M
5.2964060,25.8000000,21.5000000,1,14,2 ^M
2.8620000,21.4000000,28.9000000,1,15,2 ^M
"monet.csv" 431 lines, 16875 characters
```

As you can see, we have the header line and the prices. There's one thing that I want to point out: with some of these prices, if it they are less than a million, you'll notice that they have no leading 0 on their value, and this appears throughout the dataset. So, we are going to introduce a quick fix. First, we will remove the header line and save the file. Now, let's go back to our terminal and type the following code:

```
jcchurch@dataanalysis:~/Downloads$ sed -i 's/^\./0./' monet.csv
```

We have done a quick `sed` script. `-i` means we're going to do an in-place change on the file. Whenever we see a line beginning with an expression of a dot, we are going to replace it with a 0 dot. Now let's go and check our file, which should give us the following result:

```
3.9937800,21.3000000,25.6000000,1,1,1  ^M
8.8000000,31.9000000,25.6000000,1,2,2  ^M
0.1316940,6.9000000,15.9000000,0,3,3  ^M
2.0375000,25.7000000,32,1,4,2  ^M
1.4875000,25.7000000,32,1,4,2  ^M
1.8700000,25.6000000,31.9000000,1,4,1  ^M
```

As you can see, all of those values that had just a dot at the beginning now have a 0 at the beginning. Now let's go ahead and copy this file into our `data` folder, as shown in the following example:

```
jcchurch@dataanalysis:~/Downloads$ cp monet.csv ~/Code/HaskellDataAnalysis/data/
jcchurch@dataanalysis:~/Downloads$ 
```

Let's now go back to our notebook and play with the imports a little bit. We need to load our CSV library and also add several imports, as demonstrated in the following example:

```
In [29]:  :load DescriptiveStats
          :load MyCSV

In [30]:  import System.Random
          import Data.List
          import Data.Maybe
          import Text.CSV
          import Graphics.EasyPlot
          import DescriptiveStats
          import MyCSV
```

We have imported `Data.Maybe`, `MyCSV`, and `Text.CSV`; and that should do the trick. Now, in order to save us a little bit of time, we are going to scroll down to where we had defined the `normal` in our notebook and rerun that line. Just make sure it's still there. Now let's introduce the KDE function, as shown in the following example:

```
In [32]:  kde :: [Double] -> Maybe ([Double], [Double])
          kde [] = Nothing
          kde xs = Just (domain, mykde)
             where
                 mykde = map (/ sum shape) shape
                 shape = foldl1 (zipWith (+)) (map (\x -> (map (normal x 1) domain)) xs)
                 low = -5 + fst highlow
                 high = 5 + snd highlow
                 highlow = fromJust (range xs)
                 domain = [low,(low+0.1)..high]
```

Now, this is going to be a review of the last section. We're only passing in one dataset and we are returning a `Maybe` of two `Double` values, the first of which is the `domain` and the second of which is the `range`; and the range represents the adjusted KDE. As you recall from the last section, we are setting our low value to be whatever the low is: −5; and the high value to be whatever the high is of our domain: +5. We then just follow the steps of the KDE as we did them earlier, including the shape of the KDE divided by the sum.

Now let's go ahead and grab our data from the Monet dataset, as shown in the following example:

```
In [33]:  monet <- parseCSVFromFile "../data/monet.csv"
```

Now, we need to read those Monet prices. Hopefully you did the `sed` trick, where we added zeros to the beginning of some of those line items. If you didn't do that, then this next step isn't going to work. So, we're going to get our Monet prices, and we're going to read the index from Monet from column 0. We're going to parse these as a list of `Double`, as shown in the following code:

```
In [34]:  monetPrices = readIndex monet 0 :: [Double]
```

Without doing anything to this dataset, let's take a moment to plot what this dataset looks like, as shown in the following example:

```
In [35]:  plot X11 $ zip [1..] (sort monetPrices)
          True
```

So, we have plotted the values starting from 1, and we have sorted the Monet prices so you get a brief idea of what the smallest and largest values are. This is shown on the following graph:

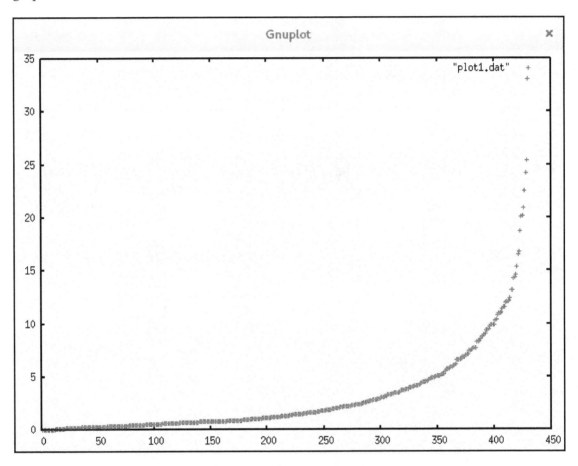

You can see here that we have over 400 observations, and that the y axis here is the value in millions. Some of these get to over 30 million dollars, but, as you can see, most of them are below 5 million dollars. It looks like 370 or so paintings are less than 5 million dollars and the rest are above 5 million. It kind of gives you an idea about the dataset distribution, but this doesn't describe the shape of the distribution, the KDE does that. So, let's compute that KDE now, as shown in the following example:

```
In [36]:  Just (domain, kdeAdj) = kde monetPrices
```

There we go. Let's go ahead and plot this, using the following code:

```
In [37]: plot X11 $ zip domain kdeAdj
         True
```

The following graph shows the actual shape of the data:

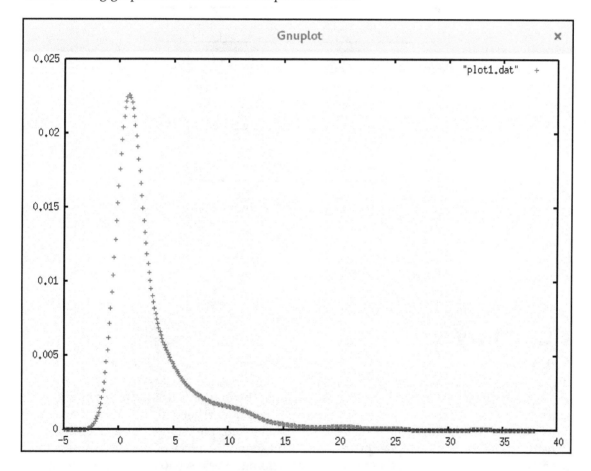

You can see that there is a strong peak in the dataset, just after 0. Now here, the x axis has shifted. We now have the x axis representing a dollar amount in millions. Right at 0, you see how our continuous function is predicting sale prices of Monet paintings that are negative.

You can essentially just cut those off after 0, but our question that we set forth at the beginning of this section is: what is the probability that a painting will sell for 5 million dollars or more? So, what we do is we figure out all of the domain values that are 5 or greater and then figure out what the corresponding probabilities are, and then add those probabilities together. So, let's find those indices in which the price of the painting is 5 or greater, as shown in the following example:

```
In [38]:  indices = findIndices (>= 5) domain
```

findIndices is a wonderful little function in the Data.List library. We're going to search for domain values greater than, or equal to, 5. We then map those to the adjusted KDE and then compute the sum of that, as demonstrated in the following code:

```
In [39]:  sum $ map (\x -> kdeAdj !! x) indices
          0.19975630172705675
```

We have passed in a function to map where we have adjusted the KDE, and whatever that x index value is from our indices list. We see that we get a probability of almost 20 % - it's almost 0.2. So, if a Monet painting ever comes up for sale in the future, there is a 0.2 probability that it will go for 5 million dollars or more. So, hopefully, that gives you an idea about the utility of the kernel density estimator.

Summary

In this chapter, we introduced the central limit theorem before we covered normal distribution. Normal distribution is a smooth, strongly peaked function where the area under the curve is 1. We discussed how the normal distribution works as an excellent kernel for the kernel density estimator. We performed the kernel density estimation on a small dataset and discussed how shape of the data looked. We then performed kernel density estimation for the Monet price dataset and found the probability of a painting going for 5 million dollars or more. Our next chapter is going to be a section review, where we accumulate all of the content that we've gone over in this book so far.

6
Course Review

In this chapter, we're going to tie together the first five chapters, using the MovieLens dataset from the University of Minnesota. We're going to cover the highlights from all of the chapters, and hopefully drop in some new content along the way. So, in this chapter we are going to cover the following topics:

- Converting CSV variation files into SQLite3
- Using SQLite3 SELECT and the DescriptiveStats module for descriptive statistics
- Creating compelling visualizations using EasyPlot
- Applying the kernel density estimator to the MovieLens dataset

Converting CSV variation files into SQLite3

In this section, we are going to be discussing CSV variations to SQLite3. CSV file stands for comma-separated values. Perhaps I mentioned in Chapter 1, *Descriptive Statistics,* about how CSV isn't really a standard, and it may come as a surprise to you that the comma-separated values do not have to be separated by commas in order to still be considered a CSV file. That's the lack of standardness there. So, in this section, we're going to be downloading the MovieLens dataset. We're going to be exploring the types of CSV file formats in this particular dataset and converting these datasets using SQLite3.

Let's go back to our machine and, in the Google search, type in MovieLens dataset. The first link in the search result will have our dataset and we want to download the MovieLens 100K dataset, as shown in the following screenshot:

MovieLens 100K Dataset

Stable benchmark dataset. 100,000 ratings from 1000 users on 1700 movies. Released 4/1998.

- README.txt
- ml-100k.zip (size: 5 MB, checksum)
- Index of unzipped files

Permalink: http://grouplens.org/datasets/movielens/100k/

Now, there are several datasets in this zipped file. MovieLens is a project at the University of Minnesota in which the researchers have asked people to rate movies on a scale of 1 to 5 with 1 being the least rating and 5 being the highest. The first 100K dataset was released back in 1998. We're going to be working with this older dataset because it's smaller. Let's download the ml-100k.zip file, go to our Download folder, unzip the file, and explore it, as shown in the following screenshot:

```
jcchurch@dataanalysis:~/Downloads$ ls
aapl.csv        earthquakes.csv  gl2015.zip    monet.csv
all_week.csv    GL2015.TXT       ml-100k.zip   usgs.sqlite3
jcchurch@dataanalysis:~/Downloads$ unzip ml-100k.zip
```

Inside the ml-100k folder you will see the following files:

```
jcchurch@dataanalysis:~/Downloads$ cd ml-100k/
jcchurch@dataanalysis:~/Downloads/ml-100k$ ls
allbut.pl  u1.base  u2.test  u4.base  u5.test  ub.base  u.genre  u.occupation
mku.sh     u1.test  u3.base  u4.test  ua.base  ub.test  u.info   u.user
README     u2.base  u3.test  u5.base  ua.test  u.data   u.item
jcchurch@dataanalysis:~/Downloads/ml-100k$ vi README
```

There is a file in our folder called README. Let's open that up. I do encourage you to read this entire file. There are guidelines on how this dataset can be used. For example, you must download it from the MovieLens site and you must not use this dataset for commercial purposes. We're using it for academic reasons, so it shouldn't be a problem. So, let's scroll down until we find the description of the file formats. The following screenshot shows the brief descriptions of the data:

```
DETAILED DESCRIPTIONS OF DATA FILES
================================================

Here are brief descriptions of the data.

ml-data.tar.gz    -- Compressed tar file.  To rebuild the u data files do this:
                  gunzip ml-data.tar.gz
                  tar xvf ml-data.tar
                  mku.sh

                                                    106,0-1        65%
```

We're looking for u.data - that is our primary file. Let's open up a new terminal, and explore u.data, as demonstrated in the following screenshot:

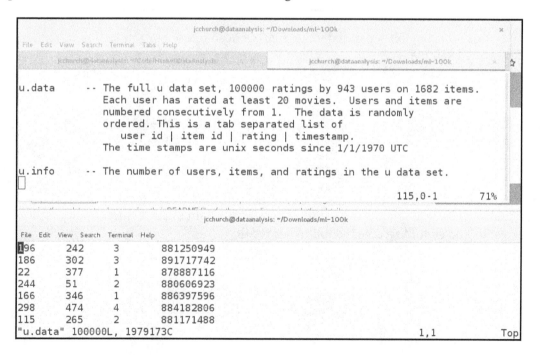

There are 100,000 ratings in this file and you can see that there are 100,000 lines in the file mentioned at the bottom of our window. So, one line represents one record. The description says that there are tabs separating the list of values, and there are four fields. And, in the terminal below, we can see that there are four fields and that they are all integers, and they represent the user ID, item ID, the rating, and the timestamp. Now, we will have to open one more terminal, hopefully you will stay with me as I jump back and forth between the two terminals. In the newly opened terminal, we're going to type in the following command:

```
jcchurch@dataanalysis:~/Downloads/ml-100k$ sqlite3 movies.sqlite3
SQLite version 3.8.7.1 2014-10-29 13:59:56
Enter ".help" for usage hints.
sqlite>
```

Here's where we'll be creating the tables. Let's create a table for our data, as demonstrated by the following command:

```
sqlite> CREATE TABLE data (userid INTEGER, itemid INTEGER, rating INTEGER, timestamp
 INTEGER);
```

Now, because this is a tab-separated value file, we need to use our mode tabs, as shown in the following example:

```
sqlite> .mode tabs
```

In the past, we've used CSV, and there's a built-in mode just for tab-separated values, and it's called **tabs**. Now we need to import our data, as shown in the following screenshot:

```
sqlite> .import u.data data
```

If all goes according to plan, you should now be able to run SELECT queries on your data. Let's test it. You should receive the following result:

```
sqlite> SELECT * FROM data LIMIT 3;
196     242     3       881250949
186     302     3       891717742
22      377     1       878887116
```

We've got the first three rows in our dataset.

Now, go to our README file and scroll down to the next file, which is u.info. We will see that it has the number of users, items, and ratings. Open the file using the terminal and you will see the following output:

```
943 users
1682 items
100000 ratings
~
~
"u.info" 3L, 36C
```

There are only three lines in the file, and it just talks about the dataset. Next up we have u.item. So, u.item includes information about the movies but they call it items, as shown in the following example:

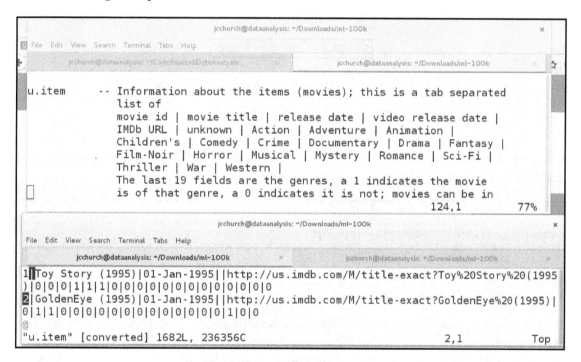

So, this is a tab-separated list, it has a lot of fields in this dataset, 19 in total. Now, you'll notice the documentation says tab separated, but, if we look down at the file itself, these are pipes rather than tabs. So, what we would like to do next is to create a table for our items. Because this is going to be a really long line, I have included it in the code files that will be provided for you along with this book so that you don't have to retype all of it.

The following example makes this clear:

```
sqlite> CREATE TABLE items (movieid INTEGER, title TEXT, releasedate TEXT, videorele
asedate TEXT, imdburl TEXT, unknown INTEGER, action INTEGER, adventure INTEGER, anim
ation INTEGER, childrens INTEGER, comedy INTEGER, crime INTEGER, documentary INTEGER
, drama INTEGER, fantasy INTEGER, filmnoir INTEGER, horror INTEGER, musical INTEGER,
 mystery INTEGER, romance INTEGER, scifi INTEGER, thriller INTEGER, war INTEGER, wes
tern INTEGER);
```

Because this is the pipe-separated file there is no built-in, pipe-separated mechanism, so we just have to declare that the separator is a pipe, as shown in the following example:

```
sqlite> .separator "|"
```

Next, we say that the mode is a list. Whenever we set up list mode, it will look for the separator field and determine how we separate our file, as shown in the following example:

```
sqlite> .mode list
```

Now, we import u.item into items, as demonstrated in the following code:

```
sqlite> .import u.item items
```

If all goes according to plan, you should have your items set up. Now we are going to select the first two items using the following command:

```
sqlite> SELECT * FROM items LIMIT 2;
1|Toy Story (1995)|01-Jan-1995||http://us.imdb.com/M/title-exact?Toy%20Story%20(1995
)|0|0|0|1|1|1|0|0|0|0|0|0|0|0|0|0|0|0|0
2|GoldenEye (1995)|01-Jan-1995||http://us.imdb.com/M/title-exact?GoldenEye%20(1995)|
0|1|1|0|0|0|0|0|0|0|0|0|0|0|0|0|1|0|0
```

Well, we got Toy Story and GoldenEye.

Let's continue looking at our README file. If you scroll down, you will see u.genre, which is just a listing of genres. We are going to skip it as it's not that interesting. Then we have u.user, which has the demographic information of all of the users interviewed by the researchers. Let's open that dataset. We should see the following screenshot:

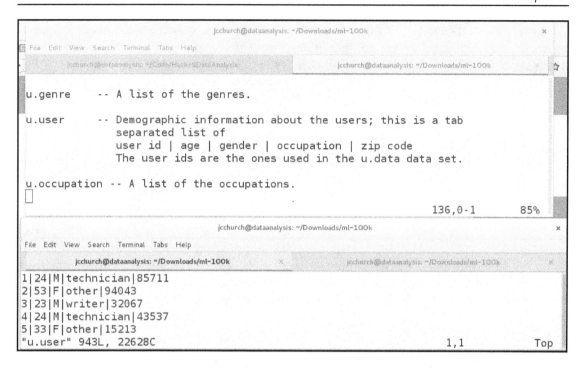

You'll see again it is another pipe-separated file, despite the fact that the documentation says it's tab. Again, we're going to create a table based on this content, as shown in the following example:

```
sqlite> CREATE TABLE users (userid INTEGER, age INTEGER, gender TEXT, occupation TEX
T, zipcode INTEGER);
```

Now we already have our mode set up for pipe-separated values, so we should just be able to do an import, as demonstrated by the following example:

```
sqlite> .import u.user users
```

Now let's do a SELECT query, as shown in the following example:

```
sqlite> SELECT * FROM users LIMIT 3;
1|24|M|technician|85711
2|53|F|other|94043
3|23|M|writer|32067
```

Alright. Next, in the README file, you have `u.occupation`, which is a list of occupations, again, we are skipping it as it is not that interesting. The remaining files in this dataset are used for machine learning projects, as shown in the following example:

```
u.occupation -- A list of the occupations.

u1.base     -- The data sets u1.base and u1.test through u5.base and u5.test
u1.test        are 80%/20% splits of the u data into training and test data.
u2.base        Each of u1, ..., u5 have disjoint test sets; this if for
u2.test        5 fold cross validation (where you repeat your experiment
u3.base        with each training and test set and average the results).
u3.test        These data sets can be generated from u.data by mku.sh.
u4.base
u4.test
                                                    144,1           91%
```

Since machine learning is not within the scope of our book we are just going to stick with the three tables that we explored in this section. So, we have our dataset set up, and I believe we're ready to go. In the next section, we're going to be using descriptive stats with SQLite3.

Using SQLite3 SELECT and the DescriptiveStats module for descriptive statistics

This section will serve as our review of the SQLite3 SELECT queries and our DescriptiveStats module. In this section, we're going to take a look at loading data from our MovieLens dataset into an IHaskell notebook. We're going to be demonstrating the built-in avg function in SQLite3 and a simple inner table join in SQLite3. We're also going to be using SQLite3 and descriptive stats to find the highest median across three genres of movies. We want to know which genre is considered the highest-rated: action, drama, or sci-fi movies. In the previous section, we had just created the `movies.sqlite3` database. What we need to do now is to copy that file into our data folder, and, if we look at this folder, we should see our `movies.sqlite3` file, as shown in the following example:

```
jcchurch@dataanalysis:~/Downloads/ml-100k$ ls
allbut.pl        u1.base  u3.base  u5.base  ub.base  u.info
mku.sh           u1.test  u3.test  u5.test  ub.test  u.item
movies.sqlite3   u2.base  u4.base  ua.base  u.data   u.occupation
README           u2.test  u4.test  ua.test  u.genre  u.user
jcchurch@dataanalysis:~/Downloads/ml-100k$ cp movies.sqlite3 ~/Code/HaskellDataAn
alysis/data/
jcchurch@dataanalysis:~/Downloads/ml-100k$ ls ~/Code/HaskellDataAnalysis/data/
GL2015.TXT  monet.csv  movies.sqlite3  stocks.sqlite3  usgs.sqlite3
jcchurch@dataanalysis:~/Downloads/ml-100k$
```

Now let's go back and create a MovieLens notebook in our IHaskell environment. Here is where we're going to study the MovieLens dataset. So, let's begin by loading our DescriptiveStats model and importing our central libraries: Data.List, Database.HDBC, Database.HDBC.SQLite3, and DescriptiveStats, as shown in the following example:

```
In [1]:  :load DescriptiveStats

In [2]:  import Data.List
         import Database.HDBC
         import Database.HDBC.Sqlite3
         import DescriptiveStats
```

Next, we need to create a connection to our database, as shown in the following example:

```
In [3]:  db <- connectSqlite3 "../data/movies.sqlite3"
```

Now, if you've used databases for any length of time, you've probably already run into the avg function for computing means. It's built into SQL. So let's go ahead and demonstrate that now, in the following way:

```
In [4]:  quickQuery db "SELECT avg(rating) FROM data" []
         [[SqlDouble 3.52986]]
```

So, we have done a quick query on our database and selected the average rating from our dataset, and we can see that the average rating is 3.53. This rating is across all movies. Now, let's change avg to say something such as median, which is another popular descriptive statistic, as shown in the following example:

```
In [5]: quickQuery db "SELECT median(rating) FROM data" []
        SqlError {seState = "", seNativeError = 1, seErrorMsg = "prepare 32: SELECT median(rating) FROM data: no such function: mec
```

We see that median doesn't exist. Let's try again, with another popular one: the mode, as shown in the following example:

```
In [6]: quickQuery db "SELECT mode(rating) FROM data" []
        SqlError {seState = "", seNativeError = 1, seErrorMsg = "prepare 30: SELECT mode(rating) FROM data: no such function: mode'
```

Again, it doesn't exist. It gives us an error. So, this addresses the importance of having a descriptive stats library, such as the one we made in Chapter 1, *Descriptive Statistics*. So, let's create a dataset consisting of all of the ratings for movies that are of the action genre. Our genre information is in the items table, but our ratings are in the data table. So, what we have to do is perform an inner join in order to align these two datasets. This is fairly straightforward to do using a little bit of SQLite3 SQL query. So, we are going to call this ratingsAction, as shown in the following screenshot:

```
In [7]: ratingsAction <- quickQuery db "SELECT data.rating FROM data, items WHERE data.itemid=items.movieid AND items.action=1" []
```

So, we have done a query on our database. We're going to do a SELECT data.ratings. Anytime we do a table join, we prefix all of our columns with the tables. So, we do table.column. In our case, it's data.rating. We're then pulling from data and items, and we want to know any place where our data.itemid field matches our items.movieid field, and where the items.action field is equal to 1.

Now let's check the length of that dataset, as shown in the following example:

```
In [8]: length ratingsAction
        25589
```

Of the 100,000 ratings in our dataset, it looks like over 25,000 ratings represent action movies. Let's create the `readColumn` partial function that we've used previously, as shown in the following example:

```
In [9]:  readColumn = map fromSql
```

So, `readColumn` is a mapping from SQL. Now, let's compute our `mean`, as shown in the following example:

```
In [10]:  mean (readColumn ( (head . transpose) ratingsAction) :: [Double])
          Just 3.480245417953027
```

We are reading in the column information. We then did a `head . transpose` of our ratings of action movies, and parsed that into a list of Doubles. As we recall from earlier, the overall average of our ratings is 3.53, but, for the action movies, it's 3.48. Let's try this again, with the `median`, as demonstrated in the following screenshot:

```
In [11]:  median (readColumn ( (head . transpose) ratingsAction) :: [Double])
          Just 4.0
```

So, we have taken our previous statement and changed the mean to median, and we see that the median is 4. Let's do this again, but, instead of action movies, let's check for drama movies. To do this, we are going to modify our earlier statements and we are going to call this `ratingsDrama`, as shown in the following example:

```
In [12]:  ratingsDrama <- quickQuery db "SELECT data.rating FROM data, items WHERE data.itemid=items.movieid AND items.drama=1" []
```

Let's compute the `mean` of our drama movies, which will give us the following result:

```
In [13]:  mean (readColumn ( (head . transpose) ratingsDrama) :: [Double])
          Just 3.6873793708484772
```

We can see it's 3.69. Now let's check the median, as demonstrated in the following example:

```
In [14]:  median (readColumn ( (head . transpose) ratingsDrama) :: [Double])
          Just 4.0
```

Once again it's 4. Finally, we will do this again for sci-fi movies, as shown in the following example:

```
In [15]:  ratingsScifi <- quickQuery db "SELECT data.rating FROM data, items WHERE data.itemid=items.movieid AND items.scifi=1" []
```

Now, let's pull our mean of the sci-fi movies, and we should see the following code:

```
In [16]:  mean (readColumn ( (head . transpose) ratingsScifi) :: [Double])
          Just 3.5607227022780834
```

We got 3.56. Finally, the median of the sci-fi movies should give us the following result:

```
In [17]:  median (readColumn ( (head . transpose) ratingsScifi) :: [Double])
          Just 4.0
```

So, we've discovered that the median rating for all three genres that we decided to look at in this video was 4, and that they all had slightly different mean values. The highest mean was from the drama category followed by the sci-fi category, and then the action category. So, more users appreciate our dramas than our sci-fi or action movies. In our next section, we will be creating compelling visualizations of the MovieLens dataset.

Creating compelling visualizations using EasyPlot

For this section, I would like to propose a question. As we get older, do our perceptions of movies increase with approval, decrease with approval, or stay about the same? In other words, what we are trying to figure out is: as we get older, do we appreciate movies more and rate them higher, do we appreciate movies less and rate them lower, or do they stay about the same? What we would like to do is pull together the data in this section, plot it, and see if we can answer that question. So, in this section, we're going to perform a table join to study age and the average movie rating. We're going to be parsing that information into a useable type for plotting, and then we're going to plot. Let's go back to our MovieLens IHaskell notebook and import `Graphics.EasyPlot`, it's a plotting library. This is shown in the following example:

```
In [1]:   :load DescriptiveStats

In [21]:  import Data.List
          import Data.Maybe
          import Database.HDBC
          import Database.HDBC.Sqlite3
          import Graphics.EasyPlot
          import DescriptiveStats
```

Because of how I stated the question, this can be done in a single SELECT query. So, let's get started. `ageRatings` is what we are going to call our result. This is shown in the following example:

```
ageRating <- quickQuery db "SELECT users.age, avg(data.rating) FROM data,
users WHERE data.userid=users.userid GROUP BY users.age" []
```

We have done a `quickQuery` on our database, where we have selected `users.age` and average of `data.rating`. We're going to rely on the `avg` function built into SQLite3 for our averaging. We have then pulled these from `data` and `users` where `data.userid` is equal to `users.userid`. At this point in our query, if we were to perform a cross-section of all of our users' ages and data ratings, then every age would have a corresponding rating; and if we were to average that corresponding rating we would just be averaging a single number, and so the averaging wouldn't really serve a purpose. What we did was to group all of those ages together, and then average that group in a batch.

Next, we need to parse the information out of our `ageRatings` variable, as shown in the following example:

```
In [23]:  age = readColumn (((!! 0) . transpose) ageRatings) :: [Double]
```

We're going to read columns on our `ageRatings`. But before we can read the age ratings directly, we need to massage that dataset a little bit. Right now it is in a column format, where the data we want is in columns. Now you can't just ask for a column in this particular two-dimensional data structure, you can only ask for a full row. So, what we can do is transpose the data, and then ask for a full row. So, we have pulled from the first row and then parsed this as a list of Doubles. Now, in our `ageRatings` table, the average ratings are going to be on the second column. Once again, you can't just grab a column, you have to transpose and pull from the second row. So, all we do is change that 0 to a 1, and change `age` to `avgRating`, as shown in the following example:

```
In [24]:  avgRating = readColumn (((!! 1) . transpose) ageRatings) :: [Double]
```

Now we need to plot. So, for that, we will use the following command:

```
In [25]:  plot X11 $ zip age avgRating
          True
```

So, we have zipped our `age` and `avgRating`, and we have our plot, as shown in the following graph:

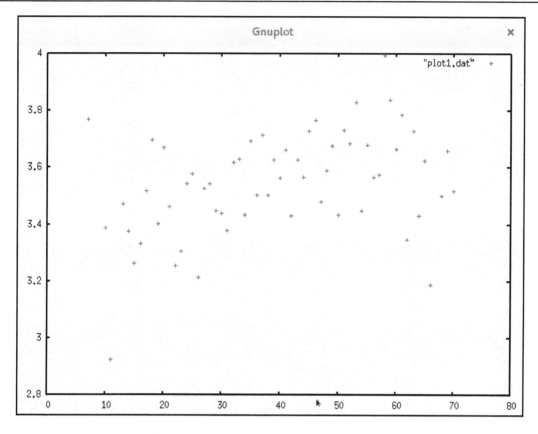

We can see a few features here. For instance, the lowest point on the graph appears to be approximately 10-year-olds, with an average rating of less than 3, and the highest rating appears to be approximately 57-year-olds, with an average rating of 4. There's another high point we can see, which is 72-year-olds with a rating of nearly 4. So, we can see that there is an upward slant to the dataset. In other words, based on looking at this graph, as we get older we tend to appreciate movies more. Now, is there any truth to this? Well, we would have to perform something called regression analysis, which is a topic for another section. For now, we're just going to have to speculate based on the direction of the data, that is, this visualization. We could improve this plot by adding a title, and we can do that as follows:

```
In [22]:  plot X11 $ Data2D [Title "Age vs Avg. Rating"] [] (zip age avgRating)
          True
```

So we have added our title and a blank list, as shown in the following graph:

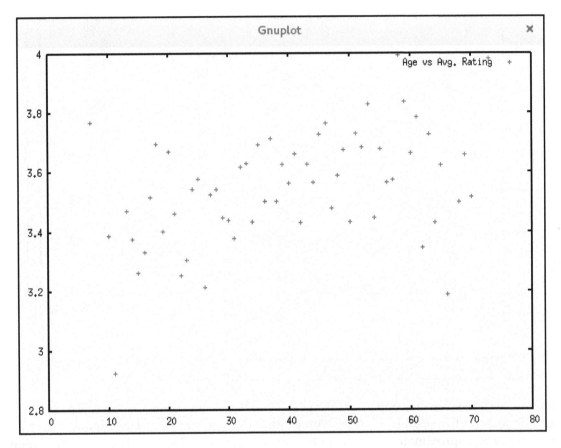

This plot seems to be publication-ready. In our next section, we will discuss kernel density estimation.

Reintroducing kernel density estimation

In this section, we reintroduce kernel density estimation (KDE). When using kernel density estimation, we are attempting to reveal the shape of a dataset with a limited amount of information. Also, in this section, we're going to investigate which movies in the dataset have the highest rating; we're going to compute the KDE of a select group of movies using their rating; and, finally, compute the KDE overlap of two movies.

Let's go back to our MovieLens dataset notebook and import `Data.Maybe`, as shown in the following example:

```
In [1]:  :load DescriptiveStats

In [33]:  import Data.List
          import Data.Maybe
          import Database.HDBC
          import Database.HDBC.Sqlite3
          import Graphics.EasyPlot
          import DescriptiveStats
```

If you recall, this library is used in our KDE function. So, we are going to use the KDE function, which is almost identical to what we saw in the last section. The one addition is that we have added a normal line to the bottom of the function, as demonstrated in the following example:

```
In [34]:  kde :: [Double] -> Maybe ([Double], [Double])
          kde [] = Nothing
          kde xs = Just (domain, mykde)
            where
                mykde = map (/ sum shape) shape
                shape = foldl1 (zipWith (+)) (map (\x -> (map (normal x 1) domain)) xs)
                low = -5 + fst highlow
                high = 5 + snd highlow
                highlow = fromJust (range xs)
                domain = [low,(low+0.1)..high]
                normal mu sd x = exp (-((x-mu)^2 / (2*sd*sd))) / sqrt (2*sd*sd*pi)
```

This is a normal kernel KDE with a standard deviation of 1. What we would like to do next is run a query that tells us which movies in our dataset have the highest ratings. Not only that, we would like to get the title of those movies based on the items dataset, as shown in the following code:

```
quickQuery db "SELECT data.itemid, items.title FROM data, items WHERE
data.itemid=items.movieid GROUP BY data.itemid ORDER BY count(data.rating)
DESC LIMIT 10" []
```

As this is going to produce a lot of data, we have limited our response to 10 records, as shown in the following example:

```
[[SqlInt64 50,SqlByteString "Star Wars (1977)"],[SqlInt64 258,SqlByteString "Contact (1997)"],[SqlInt64 100,SqlByteString
 "Fargo (1996)"],[SqlInt64 181,SqlByteString "Return of the Jedi (1983)"],[SqlInt64 294,SqlByteString "Liar Liar (1997)"]
,[SqlInt64 286,SqlByteString "English Patient, The (1996)"],[SqlInt64 288,SqlByteString "Scream (1996)"],[SqlInt64 1,SqlB
yteString "Toy Story (1995)"],[SqlInt64 300,SqlByteString "Air Force One (1997)"],[SqlInt64 121,SqlByteString "Independen
ce Day (ID4) (1996)"]]
```

So, what you see printed out on the screen are two pieces of information per record. If you recall, the two pieces of information are the `data.itemid` and the `title`. So, the data listed will be in order of what has the highest count in our dataset based on the `data.itemid`. So, data ID 50 has the most entries in our dataset, followed by 258, 100, and so on. The movies in order are *Star Wars, Contact, Fargo, Return of the Jedi,* and so on. So, next, we are going to compute the KDE of the top movie in our dataset, the one that has been reviewed the most often, in this case, *Star Wars.* So, let's pull the data out of the *Star Wars,* and we'll call this `starwarsRaw`, as shown in the following example:

```
In [36]:  starwarsRaw <- quickQuery db "SELECT rating FROM data WHERE itemid=50" []
```

So, we have done a `quickQuery` on our database and we are going to just select the rating from data where the `itemid` is equal to `50`, and that will represent *Star Wars.* Now, let's convert the `starwarsRaw` dataset into a list of Doubles. We will name this as `starwars`, as shown in the following example:

```
In [37]:  starwars = readColumn (((( !! 0) . transpose) starwarsRaw) :: [Double]
```

We are reading from the column in `starwarsRaw`. If you recall, this is a single-column dataset, but it's not easy to access that one column. So, we are going to grab the first row after our transpose. Now, let's look at the length of `starwars`, as shown in the following example:

```
In [38]:  length starwars
          583
```

There are 583 ratings for *Star Wars* in this dataset. Let's try these three steps again with a different movie, and the one I picked out is *Liar Liar*, as shown in the following example:

```
In [39]: liarliarRaw <- quickQuery db "SELECT rating FROM data WHERE itemid=294" []
```

We have changed the `itemid` from 50 to 294 as it's the ID of *Liar Liar*, and we have named it as `liarliarRaw`. Next we convert `liarliarRaw` into a list of Doubles, and name this `liarliar`, as shown in the following example:

```
In [40]: liarliar = readColumn (((!! 0) . transpose) liarliarRaw) :: [Double]
```

Finally, let's look at the length of `liarliar`, as shown in the following example:

```
In [41]: length liarliar
```

485

We got 485. So, these are two different datasets, not only in the values represented by the list but also the number of elements in that list. Next, we should compute the KDE. So, we're going to compute the KDE of *Star Wars*, followed by the KDE of the movie *Liar Liar*, as shown in the following example:

```
In [42]: Just (domainSw, mykdeSw) = kde starwars
```

It is straightforward, we have already seen this in the Chapter 5, *Kernel Density Estimation*. We'll do the same thing again for *Liar Liar*, as shown in the following example:

```
In [43]: Just (domainLL, mykdeLL) = kde liarliar
```

Next, we want to display the dataset. If you recall, the first dataset is always in red and the second dataset is always in green unless you override it, as shown in the following example:

```
In [45]: plot X11 [Data2D [Style Lines] [] (zip domainSW mykdeSW), Data2D [Style Lines] [] (zip domainLL mykdeLL)]
         True
```

So, we'll just be plotting these two lines, as shown on the following graph:

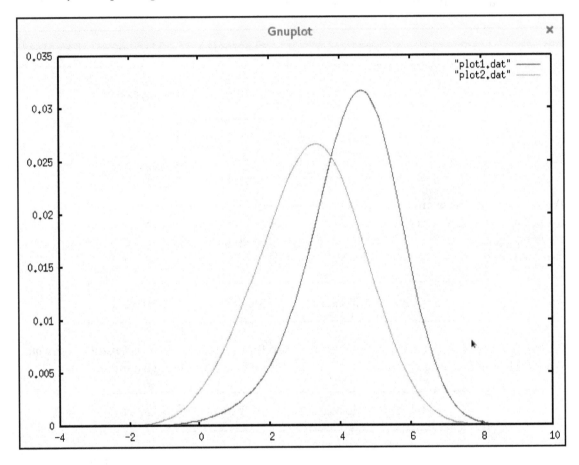

So, as you can see, the red line represents *Star Wars*. It appears to be a well-received, well-reviewed movie. Notice that the curve produced by the kernel density estimator is slanted towards the high numbers such as 4 and 5. In fact, you can make the case that it extends well past 5 on into 6, and even 8, whereas, the movie *Liar Liar* has a lagging curve behind *Star Wars*. Now, here we see two kernel density estimators for two different movies, representing two different datasets of different lengths. What we would like to do is see if we can draw a comparison between these two curves. How similar are these two curves? You can clearly see that there's some distance between the two. What we will try to do next is to measure the area formed by the triangular shape on our plot. Do you see the point where the red and green lines cross and the red line extends down to the left, while the green line extends down the right? It forms a triangular shape area, we're going to call that the overlap, and we want to find the area of that overlap. Let's close the plot and go back to our Notebook.

In order to find the area of that triangular portion in our two kernel density estimators, we first need to align the datasets. So, let's look at the domain of the two datasets. So, the domainSW for *Star Wars* is as follows:

```
In [46]:  domainSW

[-4.0,-3.9,-3.8,-3.6999999999999997,-3.5999999999999996,-3.4999999999999996,-3.3999999999999995,-3.2999999999999994,-3.19
9999999999993,-3.099999999999999,-2.999999999999999,-2.8999999999999999,-2.7999999999999999,-2.6999999999999999,-2.5999999
99999988,-2.4999999999999987,-2.3999999999999986,-2.2999999999999985,-2.1999999999999984,-2.099999999999983,-1.999999999
9999982,-1.8999999999999981,-1.7999999999999998,-1.6999999999999998,-1.5999999999999979,-1.4999999999999978,-1.39999999999
9977,-1.2999999999999976,-1.1999999999999975,-1.099999999999974,-0.999999999999973,-0.8999999999999972,-0.7999999999999
972,-0.6999999999999971,-0.599999999999997,-0.499999999999969,-0.3999999999999968,-0.2999999999999967,-0.19999999999996
62,-9.999999999999654e-2,3.5527136788005011e-15,0.10000000000000364,0.20000000000000373,0.30000000000000038,0.4000000000000
039,0.5000000000000004,0.6000000000000041,0.7000000000000042,0.8000000000000043,0.9000000000000044,1.0000000000000044,1.10
00000000000045,1.2000000000000046,1.3000000000000047,1.4000000000000048,1.5000000000000049,1.600000000000005,1.7000000000
00005,1.8000000000000052,1.9000000000000052,2.0000000000000053,2.1000000000000054,2.2000000000000055,2.3000000000000056,2
.4000000000000057,2.5000000000000058,2.600000000000006,2.700000000000006,2.800000000000006,2.900000000000006,3.0000000000
00006,3.1000000000000063,3.2000000000000064,3.3000000000000065,3.4000000000000066,3.5000000000000067,3.6000000000000068,3
.700000000000007,3.800000000000007,3.900000000000007,4.000000000000007,4.100000000000007,4.200000000000006,4.300000000000
006,4.400000000000006,4.500000000000005,4.600000000000005,4.700000000000005,4.800000000000004,4.900000000000004,5.0000000
000000036,5.100000000000003,5.200000000000003,5.300000000000025,5.400000000000002,5.500000000000002,5.600000000000001,5.
700000000000001,5.800000000000001,5.9,6.0,6.1,6.199999999999999,6.299999999999999,6.399999999999999,6.499999999999998,6.5
99999999999998,6.699999999999975,6.799999999999997,6.899999999999997,6.999999999999964,7.099999999999996,7.199999999999
996,7.299999999999995,7.399999999999995,7.499999999999995,7.599999999999994,7.699999999999994,7.799999999999994,7.8999999
99999993,7.999999999999993,8.099999999999993,8.199999999999992,8.299999999999992,8.399999999999991,8.499999999999991,8.59
9999999999999,8.699999999999999,8.799999999999999,8.899999999999999,8.99999999999999,9.099999999999989,9.199999999999989,9.29
9999999999988,9.399999999999988,9.499999999999988,9.599999999999987,9.699999999999987,9.799999999999986,9.899999999999986
,9.999999999999986]
```

As you can see it begins at −4 and extends almost to 10. Now let's look at the domain for *Liar Liar* in the following example:

```
In [47]:  domainLL

[-4.0,-3.9,-3.8,-3.6999999999999997,-3.599999999999996,-3.499999999999996,-3.399999999999995,-3.29999999999994,-3.19
99999999999993,-3.09999999999999,-2.999999999999999,-2.89999999999999,-2.79999999999999,-2.69999999999999,-2.59999999
99999988,-2.499999999999987,-2.399999999999986,-2.299999999999985,-2.199999999999984,-2.099999999999983,-1.99999999
9999982,-1.899999999999981,-1.799999999999998,-1.69999999999998,-1.599999999999979,-1.49999999999978,-1.39999999999
9977,-1.299999999999976,-1.19999999999975,-1.09999999999974,-0.9999999999973,-0.899999999999972,-0.799999999999
972,-0.699999999999971,-0.599999999999997,-0.499999999999997,-0.399999999999969,-0.299999999999967,-0.199999999996
62,-9.99999999999654e-2,3.552713678800501e-15,0.1000000000000364,0.2000000000000373,0.300000000000038,0.4000000000000
039,0.500000000000004,0.600000000000041,0.700000000000042,0.800000000000043,0.900000000000044,1.0000000000000044,1.10
00000000000045,1.200000000000046,1.300000000000047,1.400000000000048,1.500000000000049,1.600000000000005,1.7000000000
00005,1.800000000000052,1.900000000000052,2.000000000000053,2.100000000000054,2.200000000000055,2.300000000000056,2
.400000000000057,2.500000000000058,2.600000000000006,2.700000000000006,2.800000000000006,2.900000000000006,3.000000000
00006,3.100000000000063,3.200000000000064,3.300000000000065,3.400000000000066,3.500000000000067,3.600000000000068,3
.700000000000007,3.800000000000007,3.900000000000007,4.000000000000007,4.100000000000007,4.200000000000006,4.300000000000
006,4.400000000000006,4.500000000000005,4.600000000000005,4.700000000000005,4.800000000000004,4.900000000000004,5.0000000
000000036,5.100000000000003,5.200000000000003,5.300000000000025,5.400000000000002,5.500000000000002,5.600000000000001,5.
700000000000001,5.800000000000001,5.9,6.0,6.1,6.199999999999999,6.299999999999999,6.399999999999999,6.499999999999998,6.5
99999999999998,6.699999999999975,6.799999999999997,6.899999999999997,6.999999999999964,7.099999999999996,7.199999999999
996,7.299999999999995,7.399999999999995,7.499999999999995,7.599999999999994,7.699999999999994,7.799999999999994,7.8999999
99999993,7.999999999999993,8.099999999999993,8.199999999999992,8.299999999999992,8.399999999999991,8.499999999999991,8.59
9999999999999,8.699999999999999,8.799999999999999,8.899999999999999,8.999999999999999,9.099999999999989,9.199999999999989,9.29
9999999999988,9.399999999999988,9.499999999999988,9.599999999999987,9.699999999999987,9.799999999999986,9.899999999999986
,9.999999999999986]
```

This also begins at −4 and it extends almost to 10. These are identical lists. There's an easy explanation as to why these are identical: both movies had at least one 5 and at least one 1, and, because of that, the ranges are identical. The convenience of having identical ranges means that the KDEs also line up naturally; and, in order to compute the overlap of these two KDEs, we simply look for any point in which one line overlaps another line, and then we take whichever one is at the bottom. And then, after we have accumulated all of the lengths of lines that are lower than another line, we compute the sum of those. The following example shows what we're going to do:

```
In [48]:  sum $ map (\(sw, ll) -> if ll <= sw then ll else sw) (zip mykdeSW mykdeLL)

          0.6533607763536907
```

We have passed in two values, and we have called them `sw` and `ll`. If *Liar Liar* is less than or equal to *Star Wars*, then we want *Liar Liar* to be the representative line, otherwise we want *Star Wars* to be the representative one. We then have passed in our two datasets, and zipped them. So, `mykdeSW` is our first one, and `mykdeLL` is our second one. We are basically adding up all of the lines and picking out whichever one exists at the bottom, and we see that we have an overlap score of 0.65. Now, you may be asking yourself: what does this demonstrate? What is 0.65? Well, this is known as a similarity score. A similarity score judges how similar two datasets are, whereas a different score measures how different two sets are. Typically with a similarity score, a score of 1 represents that two datasets are identical. We can demonstrate this by taking our previous line, and changing the second dataset to be *Star Wars* as well, as shown in the following example:

```
In [49]:  sum $ map (\(sw, ll) -> if ll <= sw then ll else sw) (zip mykdeSW mykdeSW)
          1.0000000000000002
```

We can see that we're passing in two *Star Wars* datasets to the rest of our line, and we get, with the forgiving rounding error of Haskell, identical lines, as the result is 1. Now if we were to pass in two completely non-overlapping lines, we should get a score of 0. So, 1 means that we have lines which are perfectly similar, and 0 means we have lines which are dissimilar in every respect. Now, while there's not a lot of application here, there are many applications in math and science in which the opportunity comes to look for the similarity between two datasets; and the datasets, for whatever reason, don't have the same number of elements. But, with a little bit of work, you should be able to compute the KDEs of those two datasets, line them up along their domain (in our case, conveniently, they're already lined up on the domain), and then simply sum up all of the values that are on the bottom. If you get a value 1, or at least close to 1, then you know these two datasets are going to be very similar. So, in our case we had 65 % similarity, but I wouldn't go around saying that these are almost identical.

Summary

In this chapter, we converted a tab-separated and a pipe separated file into SQLite3. We performed a table join to combine ratings with movie genres because we have datasets that involve multiple tables, and sometimes that requires a table join. We performed a table join followed by a GROUP BY in order to study how movie ratings change with the age of the viewer. Finally, we performed KDE on individual movies and compared the two directly, despite the fact that they have different values in each dataset. So, that is the benefit of the kernel density estimator.

Other Books You May Enjoy

If you enjoyed this book, you may be interested in these other books by Packt:

Python Data Analysis - Second Edition
Armando Fandango

ISBN: 9781787127487

- Install open source Python modules such NumPy, SciPy, Pandas, stasmodels, scikit-learn,theano, keras, and tensorflow on various platforms
- Prepare and clean your data, and use it for exploratory analysis
- Manipulate your data with Pandas
- Retrieve and store your data from RDBMS, NoSQL, and distributed filesystems such as HDFS and HDF5
- Visualize your data with open source libraries such as matplotlib, bokeh, and plotly
- Learn about various machine learning methods such as supervised, unsupervised, probabilistic, and Bayesian
- Understand signal processing and time series data analysis
- Get to grips with graph processing and social network analysis

Java Data Analysis
John R. Hubbard

ISBN: 9781787285651

- Develop Java programs that analyze data sets of nearly any size, including text
- Implement important machine learning algorithms such as regression, classification, and clustering
- Interface with and apply standard open source Java libraries and APIs to analyze and visualize data
- Process data from both relational and non-relational databases and from time-series data
- Employ Java tools to visualize data in various forms
- Understand multimedia data analysis algorithms and implement them in Java.

Leave a review - let other readers know what you think

Please share your thoughts on this book with others by leaving a review on the site that you bought it from. If you purchased the book from Amazon, please leave us an honest review on this book's Amazon page. This is vital so that other potential readers can see and use your unbiased opinion to make purchasing decisions, we can understand what our customers think about our products, and our authors can see your feedback on the title that they have worked with Packt to create. It will only take a few minutes of your time, but is valuable to other potential customers, our authors, and Packt. Thank you!

Index

S

scatter plots 96, 97, 100
single variable
  line plot 71, 73, 76, 78, 79
SQLite3 SELECT
  using, for descriptive statistics 130, 132, 134
SQLite3

command line 30, 32, 33, 35
CSV variation files, converting to 123, 126, 127, 129
descriptive statistics 42, 45, 47, 48
regular expressions, working with 66, 68
working with 35, 36, 38
standard deviation 18, 19, 21